Militia Christi

ADOLF HARNACK

Militia Christi

The Christian Religion and the Military
in the First Three Centuries

Translated and Introduced by
DAVID McINNES GRACIE

FORTRESS PRESS   PHILADELPHIA

This book is a translation of *Militia Christi: Die christliche Religion und der Soldatenstand in den ersten drei Jahrhunderten,* in the 1963 edition by Wissenschaftliche Buchgesellschaft, Darmstadt, reprinted from the first edition by J. C. B. Mohr (Paul Siebeck), Tübingen, 1905.

Library of Congress Cataloging in Publication Data

Harnack, Adolf von, 1851–1930.
    Militia Christi: the Christian religion and the military in the first three centuries.

    Includes bibliographical references and index.
    Translation of: Militia Christi.
    1. Christianity and war—History of doctrines—Early church, ca. 30–600. I. Title.
BT736.2.H2913   261.8'73   81–43089
ISBN 0–8006–0673–6   AACR2

9024D81   Printed in the United States of America 1–673

Der medizinischen Fakultät
der Universität Marburg

widmet diese Blätter

□ als Zeichen ergebensten Dankes □

für die ihm verliehene Doktorwürde

der Verfasser.

Contents

Translator's Introduction

Adolf von Harnack wrote *Militia Christi* in 1905. It has never been translated into English. One wonders why not. It is an important monograph, referred to repeatedly in every subsequent study of the military question in the early church, and it was written by one of the great modern doctors of the church. Perhaps it is because Harnack's position on the question was presented in *The Mission and Expansion of Christianity in the First Three Centuries,* which he wrote in 1902 and which was translated as early as 1904.[1] But surely it is of value to have the more detailed discussion and the commentary on the sources which are assembled in *Militia Christi.* Perhaps the reason is that an English scholar, C. John Cadoux, did Harnack's work over again and then some in his book, *The Early Christian Attitude to War* (London, 1919). Cadoux was a pacifist who felt the need to present the witness of the early church against war after the Great War had been fought. W. E. Orchard, in his foreword to Cadoux's book, noted that *Militia Christi* had not yet been translated but said that he felt the present work would fill its place. Cadoux himself wrote of *Militia Christi,* "It is without doubt the most thorough and scholarly work on the subject that

---

1. See Harnack, *The Mission and Expansion of Christianity in the First Three Centuries,* 2 vols., trans. James Moffatt (New York, 1904–5), 1:385–90; 2:19–23, 204–17. The 1906 second edition was translated by Moffatt in 1908 (London: Williams & Norgate). (See 1:308–11, 414–18,' 2:52–64.) But the fourth and final edition has never been translated. Since it was written some time after *Militia Christi* and contains some new material, it should be consulted: *Die Mission und Ausbreitung des Christentums,* 2 vols. (Leipzig: Hinrichs, 1924), 1:318–20, 378–9, 428–30; 2:577–88.

has yet been produced." Yet he aimed "to present the material more proportionately and comprehensibly—and even, on a few points, more accurately than has been done by Harnack."[2]

Cadoux's pacifist leaning is quite evident in his nonetheless honest and comprehensive study of the question. Nonpacifist Christians may be said to have a bias of their own, and Cadoux felt the need to point this out in Harnack's case. Cadoux numbers Harnack among those scholars who show a striking tendency to overestimate both the degree of approval given to Christian soldiers by the early church and the extent of Christian participation in the army.[3] I think it will be helpful to the reader to list those "few points" where Cadoux thought Harnack went astray. (Page references are to my translation of *Militia Christi.*)

—He criticizes Harnack for trying to soften Tertullian's witness against military service and for regarding it as "something new, unheard of before" (p. 82).

—He thinks Harnack is wrong to conclude that there was a great divergence between theory and practice in the early church on this issue. After quoting Tertullian and Origen extensively against Christian participation in the military, Harnack wrote, "But these instructions of the moralists were in no way followed in the third century" (p. 87). "It is impossible to believe," responds Cadoux, "that the early Church swallowed this enormous compromise as easily as these modern authors would have us believe." He argues that the reverse was nearer the truth: Tertullian and Origen and others whom he quotes spoke for the general position of the church.[4]

---

2. C. John Cadoux, *The Early Christian Attitude to War* (London, 1919), pp. 10, 13. The most recent reprint is by Gordon Press (New York, 1975). See also Cadoux, *The Early Church and the World* (Edinburgh, 1925; reprint ed., Allenson), pp. 402–42.

3. Cadoux, *Early Christian Attitude,* p. 254.

4. Ibid., p. 255.

—He believes that Harnack does not give enough weight to the *Canons of Hippolytus.* This ancient order of discipline, the product of a complex development extending from the first years of the third century to far into the fifth, forbade voluntary entrance into the army to all members of the church and all baptismal candidates, while ordering those in the army not to kill. Cadoux treats the *Canons* in much more detail than Harnack did, and he concludes the following on the basis of their widespread use: "In the third century the conviction that Christianity was incompatible with the shedding of blood, either in war or in the administration of justice, was not only maintained and vigorously defended by eminent individuals like Tertullian of Carthage, Hippolytus of Rome and Origen of Palestine and Egypt, but was widely held and acted on in the Churches up and down Christendom."[5]

—He asks what grounds Harnack had for assuming that Fabius Victor, father of the martyr Maximilian, was a Christian soldier himself and that he remained so after his son's death (p. 97). This assumption tends to make Maximilian's refusal of military service the more exceptional.[6]

---

5. Ibid., pp. 127–28. The reader may consult Burton Scott Easton's translation and commentary, *The Apostolic Tradition of Hippolytus* (Hamden, Conn.: Shoe String Press, Archon Books, 1962). It is interesting that Easton (p. 26) quotes Harnack's evaluation of the *Tradition,* on which the *Canons* depend. Harnack said it is the "richest source . . . for our knowledge of the polity of the Roman Church in the oldest time, and this Roman polity may, in many regards, be accepted as the polity held everywhere." Cadoux may be right to criticize Harnack for not taking the *Canons* more seriously as a source for our knowledge of church discipline as well. But cf. Jacques Fontaine, "Christians and Military Service in the Early Church," *Concilium* 7 (1965): 116: "How far can the Canons of Hippolytus, the rigorist anti-pope, be taken in the form in which they have reached us as reflecting the Church's discipline without any further qualification? And how can one speak of *one* discipline of the Church at such an early date and particularly on such very controversial questions?"

6. Cadoux, *Early Christian Attitude,* p. 150. John Helgeland gives the best treatment of this question. Victor "held the position of *temonarius* which demanded that he either furnish a recruit for the army or collect a payment of money in his stead. . . . Apparently unable to find another

—He also questions Harnack's conclusion that Christianity was widespread in the Egyptian army based on the story in Eusebius concerning the behavior of one small squad of soldiers at the trial of a Christian (pp. 90–91).[7]

—He acknowledges that there were many Christian soldiers in the legions of Diocletian and Galerius around A.D. 300. But how many? Since they tried to purge all the Christians from the army, their number can not have been too great. Harnack is "a little inclined to overestimate the evidence."[8]

—He assigns much less weight to Canon III of the Council of Arles (A.D. 314) than Harnack does. Harnack understands it to mean that Christians were then forbidden to desert the military, and he sees this as a fundamental revision of the church's theoretical position concerning the army and war (pp. 99–101). Cadoux is less certain of its meaning, and he

---

man's son, Victor brought his own. . . . Harnack is incorrect when he states that Victor was a veteran who was required to bring his son to the army. . . . Nor is it true that Victor remained in the army after the execution of his son. If Victor was a veteran, as Harnack asserts, he would, by definition, be out of the army, even though liable to being called back in times of emergency" ("Christians and Military Service, A.D. 173–337" [Ph.D. diss., University of Chicago, 1973], p. 106).

7. Cadoux, *Early Christian Attitude,* p. 237.

8. Ibid., p. 243. But see the very interesting material in W. M. Ramsay, *Luke the Physician* (New York: Armstrong, 1908), p. 343 (reprint ed., Grand Rapids: Baker Book House, 1979). Ramsay discusses a Christian inscription of Lycaonia (ca. 338) which reveals that Maximinus Daza had ordered "that the Christians should sacrifice and should not retire from military service." He writes, "Beyond question, the reason must have been that the enforced retirement of so many Christian soldiers was weakening the army too much. It is certain that the armies of the Eastern Empire were largely composed of Christians, and Maximin found that the earlier policy was dangerous." (A reference to Ramsay is one of the added features of Harnack's fourth edition of *Mission und Ausbreitung.*) A contemporary scholar with broad knowledge of the Roman army is of the opinion that Constantine's troops were predominantly pagan. In spite of his encouragement of Christianity in the army, it remained as an enclave resistant to Christianity. See Ramsay MacMullen, *Constantine* (New York: Dial Press, 1969), pp. 133, 212.

doubts, in any case, that the decisions of the synod were generally binding.[9]

—He then marshals evidence to show that "the decision to which the leaders and majority of the Church were committed by the patronage of Constantine was very far from winning the immediate and unanimous assent of Christendom. It is evident that in many quarters the settlement was accepted only gradually and with an uneasy conscience."[10] His evidence includes the continuing use of Church Orders based on the *Canons of Hippolytus,* the witness of St. Martin of Tours in leaving the military, and St. Basil the Great's ruling that those who shed blood in war should abstain from the sacrament for three years.[11]

In an even more exhaustive study of the question, the contemporary French scholar Jean-Michel Hornus builds upon Cadoux's work and carries it further. Hornus, who also has strong pacifist convictions, first thought he would simply translate Cadoux into French but decided instead to write his own book, which he called *Evangile et Labarum* (Geneva, 1960). It has very recently been translated into English with

---

9. Cadoux, *Early Christian Attitude,* p. 256.

10. Ibid., p. 261.

11. H. Karpp, "Die Stellung der Alten Kirche zu Kriegsdienst und Krieg," *Evangelische Theologie* 17 (1957):510, agrees that Basil's rule shows a continuation of earlier discipline even in a time when the church has been united with the state. But he points out that the punishment for soldiers who kill is relatively mild, since Basil excludes a murderer for twenty years. We many add two more criticisms of Harnack by Cadoux. These appear in the latter's *Early Church and the World.* Only the first appears as an explicit criticism of Harnack. (1) He doubts we may conclude there were Christians in a certain legion whose commander was reported by Tertullian to have persecuted Christians (*Militia Christi,* p. 76). The commander may have had authority over civilians as well (*Early Church and the World,* p. 421, n. 1). (2) He says Julius Africanus, the Christian author who wrote about tactics (*Militia Christi,* p. 88), was "merely an individual curiosity, representing no one but himself." He notes that his book also contained a section on aphrodisiacs (*Early Church and the World,* p. 414).

the title *It Is Not Lawful for Me to Fight* (Scottdale, Pa.: Herald Press, 1980).[12]

Hornus argues, as Cadoux had done, that opposition to military service was not simply based on avoidance of idolatry but also the avoidance of bloodshed and violence. After many quotations from the Fathers, he comes to Hippolytus, whom he regards as the most significant witness of all. He finds in his *Canons* an essential distinction between serving in the military, which a Christian might do if compelled to, and actually fighting, which was forbidden.[13] He believes this distinction is maintained even in Canon III of the Council

---

12. Jean-Michel Hornus, *Evangile et Labarum* (Geneva, 1960), Eng. trans. *It Is Not Lawful for Me to Fight* (Scottdale, Pa.: Herald Press, 1980). This very readable translation is based on a revision of the original text completed by Hornus in 1970.

13. Hornus, p. 158. Hornus credits Henri Secrétan, "Le Christianisme des Premiers Siècles et le Service militaire," *Revue de Théologie et de Philosophie* 2 (1914):345–65, with this distinction between serving *(militare)* and fighting *(bellare)*. He thinks it provides the key to understanding passages that would otherwise appear to be contradictory. The Quaker scholar Roland Bainton, "The Early Church and War," *Harvard Theological Review* 39 (July 1946):189–211, and *Christian Attitudes to War and Peace* (Nashville: Abingdon Press, 1960), offers a similar solution. He believes that Christians were allowed to serve only to carry out police functions, not to engage in battle. He thinks the *Canons* of Hippolytus and Canon III of Arles both accommodate peacetime police duty. Stephen Gero, *"Miles Gloriosus:* The Christian and Military Service according to Tertullian," *Church History* 39 (September 1970):285, suggests that the oft-quoted phrase from Tertullian's *Apology* 42, usually translated "we serve with you in the army," may mean simply "we do service together with you," since *militare* can have that more general meaning. It does not necessarily imply violence. He quotes MacMullen, *Soldier and Civilian in the Later Roman Empire,* Historical Monographs Series, no. 52 (Cambridge, Mass.: Harvard University Press, 1963), p. 1: "Many a recruit need never have struck a blow in anger, outside a tavern." Helgeland, "Christians and Military Service, A.D. 173–337," p. 133, while acknowledging the grain of truth in MacMullen's observation, convincingly points out that police work was hardly nonviolent, since it involved raids on people's homes, battles against robbers, and the questioning (torture) of suspects. After all the scholarly review, it is interesting to note that Maximilian, in his refusal of service, did not seem to make any such distinction. He said, "mihi non licet militare, quia Christianus sum."

of Arles. Hornus is not in doubt that this canon proscribes desertion in peacetime, but this is how he understands its meaning, in considerable contrast to Harnack:

> The year 314 represents a compromise, a bargain which the Church struck with the emperor in exchange for his protection. Not only did it now allow soldiers who were in the army in peacetime to stay there; it now urged them to stay there in order to avoid scandal. In doing this, the Church carefully calculated what it took to be the lowest possible price; and in the Arles canon it held back from giving permission to kill one's neighbor. Thus, in the first official document in which the Church appeared to reject conscientious objection, it remained resolutely silent concerning conduct in wartime. For if it had said anything, it would have been compelled to give an injunction which the state would have found most uncongenial.[14]

While Hornus differs with Harnack on several points, his main debates are with other, more tendentious writers. But it was in reading Hornus' discussion of Pachomius' experience in the military that I came to note a small but significant omission in *Militia Christi.* Harnack, in listing various Christians who served in the army, mentions Pachomius, the founder of monasticism, stating that he "served in the army of Constantine against Maxentius. The love that was evidenced by Christian soldiers was said to have led him to Christianity" (p. 98). Hornus makes a great point of the fact that Pacho-

---

14. Hornus, p. 177. Gero, p. 285, finds this exegesis "bizarre." Cf. Fontaine, p. 116, who gives a general warning against Hornus. After praising his book as a mine of texts and references, he says that "the ancient texts have been conscripted into a misdirected crusade." But Karpp, p. 510, reads the canon much the same way Hornus does: "by adding 'in pace' the church continues to maintain that the avoidance of killing is the duty of a Christian or at least his right." Hans von Campenhausen is of the same opinion. See his "Christians and Military Service in the Early Church," in *Tradition and Life in the Church: Essays and Lectures in Church History* (London: William Collins Sons & Co.; Philadelphia: Fortress Press, 1968), p. 168.

mius was with Christians who were forced recruits and were in prison because they refused to fight. He quotes E. Misset: "These were simply catechumens or baptized Christians who were subject to the Church's disciplinary regulation of the time."[15] This may be reading too much into the sketchy account in *The Life of Pachomius,* but it is clear that Pachomius was a forced recruit imprisoned with other forced recruits.[16] Harnack could have been more candid.

We can thank Cadoux and Hornus for raising some red flags before the reader of *Militia Christi.* If one wishes to read an author who treats the same material with what may be termed an antipacifist bias, E. A. Ryan, S.J., may be recommended.[17] He thinks idolatry was the main barrier to Christian military service and thus believes "Constantine did not cause the Church to abandon its principles in the matter. His conversion so changed the concomitants of military service that the former more or less general disapprobation could safely be altered."[18] Tertullian, Origen, Hippolytus he labels pacifists, along with Marcion. Origen had doubtless "been too deeply affected by the counsels recommending meekness, as he had been by some other counsels."[19] He argues from silence by noting that there is "no record of any conciliar decree against military service for the entire pre-Constantinean period; not even at Elvira, where intransigence was so pronounced." He thinks Harnack is right to see this as a watchful, waiting policy on the part of the episcopate. As soon as tolerance is granted, the church rallies to

---

15. E. Misset, *Pourquoi St. Martin refusa-t-il de combattre* (Paris, 1907), p. 12.

16. See *The Life of Pachomius,* trans. Apostolos N. Athanassakis (Missoula, Mont.: Scholars Press, 1975), p. 7. Hornus' discussion of Pachomius appears on pp. 141–42.

17. E. J. Ryan, S.J., "The Rejection of Military Service by the Early Christians," *Theological Studies* 13 (March 1952):1–29.

18. Ibid., p. 3.

19. Ibid., p. 14.

support the government. This was demonstrated at Arles.[20] Ryan finds no fault with Harnack. Seen next to Ryan, Harnack seems very objective indeed.

Scholarship on this question can easily be divided between hawks and doves, with excesses committed on both sides.[21] The most recent complete study of which I am aware is by John Helgeland, who is very critical of all previous authors because of their preconceived notions.[22] Helgeland finds for the conclusions if not the methods of the hawks, arguing that the objections to enlistment had to do with official and unofficial pagan religious observances in the legions and not pacifist sentiments. It is interesting that he puts Harnack and Cadoux in the same category as believers in a fall from a pristine Christianity based on the teachings of Jesus. "Both Harnack and Cadoux have the utmost respect for the religion and ethics of Jesus and both have the notion that the Church departed from Jesus' stance on the question of bloodshed. However, they disagree concerning the time when the period of decay set in; for Harnack it is relatively early, for Cadoux it is somewhat later."[23]

---

20. Ibid., p. 27.

21. Cadoux's contemporary James Moffatt provides an example of hawkish excess in his article "War," in vol. 2 of the *Dictionary of the Apostolic Church* (Edinburgh, 1918), p. 667, when he assails Tertullian's and Origen's "fanatical anti-civic repudiation of force," which to his mind reveals a Gnostic and Manichaean bent. Cadoux himself gets carried away in his criticism of the German Roman Catholic scholar Andreas Bigelmair, who in his *Die Beteiligung der Christen am öffentlichen Leben in vorkonstantinischer Zeit* (Munich, 1902) does not even mention Maximilian. "He is certainly an awkward martyr for a Romanist to deal with, but doubly so for one who is both a Romanist and a German" (*Early Christian Attitude*, p. 150, n. 1).

22. Helgeland, "Christians and Military Service, A.D. 173–337." On pp. 6–32 he reviews the literature since 1900 and notes the ideological lineup. He briefly summarizes the findings of his unpublished dissertation in Helgeland, "Christians and the Roman Army, A.D. 173–337," *Church History* 43 (June 1974):149–61.

23. Helgeland, "Christians and Military Service, A.D. 173–337," p. 17.

Helgeland does not like "fall" theories, and he forces us to consider the very mixed state of affairs which prevailed. He calls attention to the Apocryphal Gospels, which were very popular and which presented a Jesus of power and vengeance quite different from the Jesus of the Sermon on the Mount.[24] These Gospels, he believes, would have had more influence on the ordinary Christian than the teachings of the theologians.

In fact, he so completely removes the tension that he can express the view that Canon III of Arles was probably not even necessary.[25] Military service at that time was "not very problematic for whatever reason."[26]

For Harnack, the term *militia Christi* is initially a paradox. Helgeland's presuppositionless approach to the study of this question destroys the paradox by refusing to presuppose even the teachings of Jesus in the canonical Gospels as normative for most Christians. But must we not assume that in the debate on this issue in the early church, those like Tertullian who could appeal directly to words of Jesus had some kind of edge? How shall one answer Tertullian's questions after all? "Shall it be held lawful to make an occupation of the sword, when the Lord proclaims that he who uses the sword shall perish by the sword? And shall the son of peace take part in the battle when it does not become him even to sue at law? And shall he apply the chain, and the prison, and the torture, and the punishment, who is not the avenger even of his own wrongs?"[27]

---

24. Ibid., pp. 82–85.
25. Ibid., p. 194.
26. Ibid., p. 167.
27. *The Chaplet* or *De Corona* 11, in *The Ante-Nicene Fathers: Translations of the Writings of the Fathers Down to 325 A.D.,* 10 vols., ed. Alexander Roberts and James Donaldson (American ed., Buffalo, 1886; reprint ed., Grand Rapids: William B. Eerdmans Publishing Co., 1969) (hereafter, *ANF*), 3:99. We should not leave Helgeland's dissertation without noting his review of the inscriptions (pp. 126–30), because it points to a gap in

All of this discussion has been concerned with chapter 2 of *Militia Christi,* "The Christian Religion and the Military Profession." Chapter 1, "The Christian as Soldier," has not drawn nearly as much scholarly attention. Here Harnack presents a collection of examples of the use of military terms and images in the New Testament and early Christian writings. He then suggests that this kind of language prepared the way for Christian holy wars (p. 63). Symbols and forms have their own logic, he argues. "At first unnoticeably, but soon even more clearly, the warlike element which was accepted as a symbol ushers in the reality itself, and the 'spiritual weapons of knighthood' become carnal" (p. 32).

In this first chapter, Harnack also offers an interesting insight into the influence of apocalyptic. He says that "apocalyptic contributed to the fact that Christians did not completely bar themselves from war" (p. 35). If God himself will conduct a war at the last day, then war must have its place.

Chapter 1 should be read with due caution, however. First, it should be noted that metaphors of warfare were neither original with New Testament writers and the Fathers nor limited to them. Hilarius Edmonds, O.S.B., has shown how the concept of the *militia spiritualis* was used by Plato and then the Stoics to describe the life of man, especially the life of the philosopher.[28] James Moffatt had earlier done the

---

Harnack's work. Harnack knew of no inscription in which a Christian was identified as a soldier prior to the time of Constantine (*Militia Christi,* p. 107). H. LeClercq recorded a number of such inscriptions in his article "Militarisme," in *Dictionnaire D'Archéologie Chrétienne et de Liturgie* (Paris, 1933), pp. 1155–79. Of these, Helgeland believes that seven are definitely pre-Constantinean, and he adds one more to the list. Cf. the discussion of inscriptions in Bernard Schöpf, *Das Tötungsrecht bei den frühchristlichen Schriftstellern* (Regensburg, 1958), p. 234.

28. Hilarius Edmonds, O.S.B., "Geistlicher Kriegsdienst," printed as an appendix to the 1963 Darmstadt (Wissenschaftliche Buchgesellschaft) edition of *Militia Christi.*

19

same and added a review of the use of such terms in the mystery religions.[29] Ramsay MacMullen has shown the tremendous effect of the military on all aspects of Roman life and culture in the Late Empire. For example, even in the civil bureaucracy "the lowest scribbler wore a military belt, was called a *miles,* and after the completion of his *militia, veteranus.*"[30] Stephen Gero cites this passage and suggests with reference to Harnack's work: "It is thus likely that military terminology as it became current also became trite. Perhaps *militia Christi* did not have quite the emotive value we might think it possessed."[31]

Second, we must recognize that images and symbols possess no overwhelming power over human conduct. They can be used with opposite meanings under different social conditions and in the light of different convictions. Harnack himself points to the Salvation Army as a completely militarized yet completely peaceful manifestation of the church (p. 31). Only recently in our own experience some pacifist Christians were using the image of "the Lamb's war" to describe their nonviolent opposition to the war in Vietnam, while other Christians not only supported that conflict but called it (incredibly) "Christ's war." When it came down to it, Harnack supported the military actions of his fatherland in World War I.[32] This decision had little to do with martial metaphors in the patristic literature or the Lutheran hymnal, although the use of such images in worship must have made it somewhat easier for Christians on both sides to go to war without seeing any major contradiction to their faith.

Harnack's discussion of military imagery is valued and used in a different way by Hans-Ruedi Weber in *The Mili-*

---

29. Moffatt, "War," pp. 657–58, 659–60.
30. MacMullen, *Soldier and Civilian,* p. 164.
31. Gero, p. 288.
32. See the biography *Adolf von Harnack,* by Agnes von Zahn-Harnack (Berlin, 1936), pp. 443ff. (2d ed. Berlin: de Gruyter, 1951).

tant Ministry (Philadelphia: Fortress Press, 1963). Weber is a great advocate of lay ministry and believes the military images make clear that the Christian is involved in combat with the forces of evil. But he points out how an improper use of the military terminology has led to the separation of clergy and religious from the laity. Lay Christians thus become half-committed civilians "with a staff of professional officers and some troops of mercenaries."[33]

I have prepared this translation having in mind those general students of theology and church history who are not proficient in German. I also believe that Harnack's collection of the early texts will be of value to those members of the church who continue to struggle with the military question as it affects their own lives. I think particularly of the young men and women who consider the possibility of conscientious objection to military service. The underlying issues have not changed since the first three centuries. On the one hand are the responsibilities of citizenship, on the other the need to avoid, if possible, violence, bloodshed, and idolatry of the state.

My assumption is that many of these readers will also rely on standard English translations of the early Christian literature. Therefore I have used the standard translations whenever available. When these translations differ in any significant way from Harnack's own rendering of the Greek and Latin, I have tried to indicate the same.

Quotations from the Fathers are ordinarily from *The Ante-Nicene Fathers: Translations of the Writings of the Fathers Down to 325 A.D.*, 10 vols., ed. Alexander Roberts and James Donaldson (American ed., Buffalo, 1886; reprint ed., Grand Rapids: William B. Eerdmans Publishing Co., 1969). Quotations from the apocryphal literature are from Edgar Hen-

---

33. Hans-Ruedi Weber, *The Militant Ministry* (Philadelphia: Fortress Press, 1963), p. 10.

necke, *New Testament Apocrypha,* ed. Wilhelm Schnee-melcher, trans. R. McL. Wilson (London, 1965; Amer. ed. Philadelphia: Westminster Press, 1963–65). Quotations from Eusebius are from *A Select Library of Nicene and Post-Nicene Fathers,* second series, ed. Schaff and Wace (New York, 1890; reprint ed., Grand Rapids: William B. Eerdmans Publishing Co., 1953).

Whenever a source does not appear in a standard English text, the translation is from original Greek or Latin if it so appears in *Militia Christi*; otherwise, from the German of Harnack. The titles of the early Christian writings are presented for the most part as Harnack cited them, unless a standard English translation is followed, in which case the title is identical with that found in, for example, *The Ante-Nicene Fathers.* The footnotes are unexpanded translations except for the addition of references to the sources of English translations and translator's notes. All such added material by the translator is in brackets. Harnack prepared an appendix for *Militia Christi* which contains a good number of the patristic and other quotations in the original languages. For this appendix the reader is referred to the Darmstadt 1963 reprint of *Militia Christi,* which is available in many libraries. Harnack's subject index has also been eliminated, while his index of passages has been redone to follow the rule for titles stated above.

The Lutheran Theological Seminary in Philadelphia accepted this translation and introduction as my master's thesis in their S.T.M. program. Dr. Clarence Lee kindly translated Greek and Latin passages for me and Dr. Helmut Lehmann offered several suggestions to improve my translation from the German. In addition to thanking my professors at the seminary, I wish to express my gratitude for the continuing education program of the Episcopal Diocese of Pennsylvania, which made this time of study possible for me.

D. McI. G.

Preface

The problems examined in both of the following essays were briefly discussed in my work entitled *Die Mission und Ausbreitung des Christentums in den ersten drei Jahrhunderten* (1902), pp. 297ff. and 388ff.[1] They appeared to me even then to deserve a more thorough treatment, but I could not provide it within the limits of the history of mission. Here it is accomplished. I have confined myself strictly to the theme, since I am not in a position to bring something new to the more general questions like religion in the Roman army or the judgment on war and the warrior caste in the works of Greek and Roman philosophers, and I do not simply want to repeat what is known. But one must always keep the background in view if one undertakes to evaluate the special problem of the relationship of the church to the military. Tertullian wrote, "The religion of the Romans is totally of the camp; it worships the standards *(signa);* it swears by the standards; it elevates the standards above all the gods."[2] But neither should the disparaging judgments of the philosophers concerning military service be forgotten. For Christianity was not only reckoned as "philosophy" but chose to be related to philosophy and was influenced by it.

In the relationship of early Christianity to war and to the

---

1. [*The Mission and Expansion of Christianity in the First Three Centuries,* trans. James Moffatt (London: Williams & Norgate, 1908), 1:414–18, 2:52–64.]

2. [*Apology* 16, editor's translation. For a different English translation see *ANF,* 3:31.]

army, one will be amazed once more by the church's unparalleled elasticity and universalism. The church upheld the highest ideals but still established itself in the world. It understood how to derive a conservative motive for worldly living from a future hope which was quite world-forsaking. And it proved here once again that it was able to endure antagonistic forces even while it encircled them. It was already a world church while it still stood defenseless against the world.

The special justification for developing this theme of the relationship of the Christian religion to the army in a monograph lies in the facts that the early Christians (especially in the West) perceived themselves as God's soldiers and that the historical shift from paganism to Christianity first took place publicly in the army.

Bigelmair has written a study on the position of Christians toward military service in the book *Die Beteiligung der Christen am öffentlichen Leben in vorkonstantinischer Zeit* (Munich, 1902), pp. 164–201. Just now, when the type for these pages was practically set, I received de Jong's treatise, *Dienstweigering bij de oude Christenen* (Leiden, 1905). Both examinations are solid and stimulating, especially the first. I hope, however, that my own work will not be superfluous alongside theirs, since in those books the *militia Christi* is scarcely touched upon, and they have not striven throughout for completeness of material and viewpoint.

Berlin, March 20, 1905   A. H.

"The Christian Religion and the Military"—this title encompasses three problems: (1) Has the Christian religion continuously or at any time in its history assumed a warlike character and preached the right and duty of the holy war? (2) Has the church, occasionally or continuously, adopted military organization (in a transferred sense) and disciplined its believers, or a part of them, as soldiers of Christ? (3) What position has the church taken with regard to the secular military profession and to war? Has it regarded them as valid, or tolerated them, or has it condemned them? These are three different questions, but they stand in a close relationship to each other. They will be answered in the following work with respect to the first three centuries of Christianity. The first and second questions are treated together in one investigation; the third is handled separately. Whoever wishes to take these questions through the following centuries to the present day may also count upon interesting insights and worthwhile findings. What is discussed here is only intended to lay the groundwork.

[A. H.]

1

The Christian as Soldier

Militia Christi, militia dei vivi ("army of Christ, army of the living God"): the view which undergirds these concepts apparently could only have very limited range in the early Christian religion. Sayings of Jesus point in a quite different direction, and the nature of the gospel itself as it must have been understood by the first generation appears to be opposed to everything warlike. Patience, meekness, readiness for service, renunciation of one's own right—these are the virtues which ought to distinguish the Christian; even self-defense was not recognized. Those who endure injustice are called blessed, the meek are promised the inheritance of the earthly realm, peace is proclaimed to all people, and the gospel itself is called "the gospel of peace." The disciples of Jesus are not to behave the way the mighty and powerful do; their attitude is supposed to be opposite to the attitude of the ones who rule. We need say nothing more to confirm that the gospel excluded all force and had nothing warlike about it, nor would it endure the same. How apparently unnecessary it was to speak the words of Matt. 26:52 (although it certainly was necessary): "Put up your sword, for he who takes the sword will perish by the sword." And to this is connected the message that the Father in heaven does not want to carry out his work on earth by means of legions of warrior angels. (See also John 18:36.)

Yet war is one of the basic forms of all life, and there are inalienable virtues which find their highest expression at least symbolically in the warrior's calling: obedience and courage, loyalty unto death, self-abnegation and strength *(virtus)*. No higher religion can do without the images which are taken from war, and on this account it cannot dispense with "warriors." Whether a religion allows itself to be determined by these necessities, by becoming engaged more and more in the military and its forms, is a question the answer to which always reveals an important part of the history of religion. The fact that our study of the history of Christianity has until now gone into this dimension so little[1] is only a proof that we have still not completely surveyed the aspects under which religion is to be considered.

But the relationship of the higher religions to matters of war is important also from another angle. Each of these religions developed from lower stages, and on those lower stages the connection of religion to war was very close. In those religions in which the religious and the political goals come together as one, all *religiosi* are also *milites* and war is the *ultima ratio* of religion. It is always "holy war." The Jewish religion in a certain historical stage of development (a stage of long duration) was constituted no differently. Since the Christian religion developed from the Jewish, it is a priori probable that it would retain traces of the older, warlike ways.

Finally, we must remember that among the sayings of Jesus which the Evangelists have transmitted there are a few which sound warlike: "I am not come to bring peace but a sword." "The kingdom of heaven has been coming violently, and men of violence take it by force" (RSV). Add to these the obscure saying at the Last Supper, that one should sell one's mantle and buy a sword. We shall also see that the word of Jesus that one should leave all for his sake and the confession of faith in him at baptism could be conceived to be similar to

---

1. However, see the suggestions in my *Mission und Ausbreitung des Christentums in den ersten drei Jahrhunderten*, 1902, pp. 297ff. [*The Mission and Expansion of Christianity in the First Three Centuries*, trans. James Moffatt (London: Williams & Norgate, 1908), 1:414ff.]

a military oath of allegiance. To the extent that the sayings of Jesus were later torn from their historical contexts, those which sounded warlike would gain more latitude than they originally possessed.[2]

Looking away now from the beginnings toward circumstances of the present day, we become aware of the following: (1) In the Eastern churches the people (eventually also the state) and the religion grew together again so that in cases of emergency holy war was proclaimed to arouse the people to the defense of the "national god." But even without proclamations, the Russians, the Armenians, and others perceived themselves to be warriors of God if their church or nation was attacked. Even the Eastern priest or monk lifted up the cross and incited his faithful compatriots to holy

---

2. How the saying (Matt. 10:34) "I am not come to bring peace but a sword" is to be understood we learn from the context and from Luke 12:49–53. What is meant is the division within families which results from the proclamation of the gospel. Peace in this context means peace in the household. The saying that now men of violence take the kingdom of heaven by force (Matt. 11:12; cf. Luke 16:16) has been understood in different ways. Some say that Jesus speaks about this fact disapprovingly; others explain that what is happening has his approval. I do not doubt that the latter view is correct. (That is quite certain as soon as one translates v. 12a not "the kingdom of heaven suffers violence" but "the kingdom of heaven is coming with force.") Given the context, the other explanation is too complicated. The meaning is that because the kingdom of heaven now breaks in with force one must forcibly take hold of it in order to win it for oneself and not let it go by. There is something warlike in the image but not in the reality. In Luke 22:36, Jesus says that he who has no sword should sell his mantle and buy one. This admonition is indeed obscure along with the surprising addition: "And they said, 'Look, Lord, here are two swords.' And he said to them, 'It is enough'" (RSV). The most likely meaning is that Jesus is teaching his disciples about how their situation is going to change completely. As long as he was with them, he protected them from want. Now, however, there will not only be want but most bitter persecution. Against this they will have to strain every nerve, and the sword will be their most necessary implement in the future. He meant by this a warlike readiness to defend the gospel by all means; they, however, understood him literally and pointed out the two swords which were in the room. He broke off the conversation ironically with the words "It is enough." Even this explanation is not quite satisfying, for one is not prepared at the outset to understand the sword figuratively.

war. (2) The Western church also carried on holy wars in the name of Christ as long as it was tied to the state as the Eastern church was. We need only recall the wars of Charlemagne and the Crusades. There were also the wars which the papacy conducted in alliance with other states against the emperor or against other princes. Even if we exclude the campaigns which the popes led as heads of the papal states, we still find that into modern times warfare has been formally undertaken for Christ and the church. It has only been since the middle of the seventeenth century that the papacy and the Roman church (apart from the papal states) have had to operate as a peaceful power. They have had to limit themselves to politics and thereby renounce the *ultima ratio* of politics. Still, attempts have been made down to the most recent times to designate this or that war as a "war of religion" and to incite the soldiers with this thought. In the institutions of the Roman church the military element *(das militärische Element)* is present in a figurative sense in two places: (*a*) Even though in the common teaching on the sacraments (for example, *Catech. Rom.* P. II c. 1 qu. 2) the military sense of "sacrament," that is, "military oath,"[3] is now viewed with disfavor, contrary to an earlier tradition, it is still asserted of confirmation that through that sacrament the Christian begins to become a "perfect soldier of Christ."[4] Each Christian should therefore know and feel himself to be a combatant

---

3. [See below, pp. 53 ff.]
4. *Catech. Rom.* P. II, c. 3, qu. 2: "He who has been baptized, when he is anointed by the bishop with the sacred chrism . . . begins to be a stronger, even a perfect soldier, through a new and firmer virtue." A sermon from the fifth or sixth century states, "In baptism we are regenerated for life, after baptism we are confirmed for battle." In another sermon, wrongly attributed to Eusebius of Emesa, it is said that the laying on of hands and confirmation are not superfluous in spite of baptism, because "if the military order requires that when the emperor receives anyone into the army he not only designates the recruit [a soldier] but also equips him for fighting through a mastery of the weapons of war, so also the baptized one is armed in the blessing: you have made him a soldier; give him the means of war."

for Christ. (*b*) The ascetics and monks are regarded in a special way as Christ's warriors. Some of the most important orders, not to mention the medieval orders of knights, are given a military organization and understand themselves as defense troops for God, the church, and especially the pope. Much more important, however, is the theory which the Roman church has spun out of Luke 22:38, that Jesus gave the church two swords, the spiritual and the secular, and that the church is thus the possessor of all power. (3) The military element is quite far removed from the Protestant churches since the political plays a much narrower role in them than in the Catholic churches. Yet even the reformed churches found it necessary to draw the sword for the gospel in the time of the Reformation and Counter-Reformation. One thinks of the Huguenots and the armies of Cromwell; but they were passing necessities. The military has found expression in Protestantism in a quite peaceful way in an isolated phenomenon of our day. The spiritual imitation of the military is in this instance carried farther than it was in the Western monastic orders. I refer to the Salvation Army, a product of Methodism, which practices the Christianizing of "Christendom" in the form of an organization and with means (including religious language) which are patterned on the military to an objectionable degree. But they have achieved great things, and from their successes they may claim the right to their own peculiar constitution. This uniformed, tactically trained, battle-ready, but quite peaceful *militia Christi* is the most remarkable phenomenon of the organization of Christians in the present day. Finally, and in contrast to all, we must point to the Mennonites, a Christian fellowship formed from the medieval sects of the Anabaptists in the time of the Reformation. They condemn every war in principle and in practice, and they strongly forbid their members to participate in the military.

Priests and warriors, monks and warriors—one can place the whole history of the world under these headings, as Hans

31

Delbrück has shown in a spirited presentation. They are opposites, or poles, which at once repel and attract. If the forms of the military estate are transferred to the higher religions, it appears that what is warlike is turned around and changed into its strict opposite or transformed into a mere symbol. But the form has its own logic and its necessary consequences. At first unnoticeably, but soon ever more clearly, the warlike element which was accepted as a symbol ushers in the reality itself, and the "spiritual weapons of knighthood" become carnal. Even where the process does not go so far, a warlike mood enters which threatens the norm of gentleness and peace. The bellicose champion of orthodoxy is as well known in the history of the church as the aggressive ascetic and pietist. They believe that they are fighting the battles of the Lord, and they try to inflict frightful wounds. The history of "the watchmen of Zion" *(der Zionswächter)* is the darkest chapter of church history.

We limit ourselves here to the task of investigating what latitude was given to the warlike element in the earliest development of the Christian religion.

At the time that Christianity was freeing itself from the mother's womb of the Jewish religion, the warlike element was present in the latter in a double form: First, within the messianic expectation and dogma it lived in its original way and incited the Jews to warlike deeds until the uprising in the great Jewish War and beyond. Second, in the language of the prophets and psalmists this element was effective in an allegorical sense and blossomed in numerous images (spiritual battle, spiritual weaponry, and so forth).

Both are to be found again in earliest Christianity. The apocalyptic eschatology shows traces of the warlike messiah transferred to Jesus, and in the ethical admonitions images of war are found from the start.

As far as the first is concerned, one notices that the warlike element is entirely limited to apocalyptic eschatology and does not extend to the picture of Christ outside of that context. Eph. 4:8 is an exception when it says of Jesus, "When he ascended on high he led a host of captives, and he gave gifts to men" (RSV). But in essence even this passage is not an exception, for with his ascension his new form of existence already begins; he is the warlike hero who will come again. However, the hosts which will then accompany him and fight under his direction are not made up of men but of angels. The great battle and victory comes for the benefit of men, but they are not in this context *milites Christi*. Consequently, the mood of the faithful was not warlike, or rather it was warlike in a passive sense. The Jew in the last extremity really drew the sword and thus anticipated the Messiah; he had a land, a holy city, and a temple to defend. The Christian, however, was told to wait for his *Christus victor*. Certainly his fantasy filled itself with warlike pictures of hate and revenge, as the Apocalypse of John shows; but he must always have patience and longingly look forward to the moment when he would be the spectator of the great battle and victory. The inner ethical disposition which resulted from this could be more unhealthy and pernicious than if he himself had taken the sword. However, in contrast to the ruling critical point of view today, it appears to me that we tend to overestimate the significance of eschatology here as in other respects; and this messianic picture of the future has been overestimated too. If one surveys early Christian literature in its totality and looks therein for a picture of the inner disposition and bearing of the earliest Christians, and then adds to this their outward behavior, eschatology cannot be brought too much into the foreground. We should also remember the psychological fact that the world of fantasy and the world of real life are separated and that it is possible for a very calm and peaceable man to indulge at times in extravagant fantasies without having those fantasies influence his inner bearing in any essential way. History testifies that the warlike Jesus Christus Redivivus of apocalyptic never turned Christians of the first three centuries into warlike revolutionaries; to the extent that the military element entered into the Christian disposition, it is not to be traced to this source. The concept of the army of Christ to which the Christian is called had nothing to do with the warlike Christ of the future, because, as we noted, his armies were the angels. This observation is weightier than any other which could be made on this topic. Nor did the Apocalypse of John simply present Jesus Christ as a hero of war and a victor, but ever and again between those images is introduced the image of the Lamb that was slain, the Lamb with the deadly wound, and in the middle of its scenes of war we find peaceful prospects. So no one can doubt that that fantastic warlike vision is not the last word of the Christian writer of apocalyptic, let alone of Christian preaching. "The Spirit and the Bride say, 'Come.' And let him who hears say, 'Come.' And let him who is thirsty come, let him who desires take the water of life without price" (RSV). That is the last word, which expresses the assurance and the yearning of the prophets.

But the apocalyptic writings with their images of war have had an extremely important consequence. We will see that the Christian ethic generally prohibited Christian participation in war but that complete certainty about this was never achieved, and the prohibition was not really upheld. How can we explain this? In my opinion the answer that the world is stronger than Christ is not sufficient. At least at the beginning Christians were free enough of the world to submit themselves to a hard commandment. But a general rejection of war could not succeed because God himself, according to the outlook of the earliest Christians, caused wars and led them. He had done it earlier through Joshua and David. He did it in their own day through the defeat of the Jewish people and the destruction of Jerusalem, and he would do it in the future through the returning Christ. How can one reject wars generally and in every sense if God himself brings them about and leads them? Apparently there are necessary and just wars! The war at the end of days would be precisely such a war. If this is the case, then the Christian's attitude about war could not be absolute even if he was not allowed to go into the field. For that reason the prohibition could not be securely maintained, for such prohibitions can only be carried out if they are regarded as unconditional and when what is forbidden is portrayed as in every sense detestable. In this way apocalyptic contributed to the fact that Christians did not completely bar themselves from war. However, as mentioned above, it was not from apocalyptic that the consciousness of being *milites Christi* was born.

We must turn to the ethical admonitions if we want to clarify the history of the warlike element in the early church, for it developed only in them. We encounter immediately with Paul[5] a number of warlike-sounding admonitions and images (1 Thess. 5:8; 2 Cor. 6:7; Rom. 6:13–14, 23; 13:12; Eph. 6:10–18),[6] and we see that they have their origin in the images of the Old Testament prophets. This is particularly clear with the most extended allegory of this kind (Eph. 6:10–18).[7] But even its detailed execution shows at once that

---

5. Also in Revelation. The admonition in 2:10 employs a military image: "Be faithful unto death, and I will give you the crown of life" (RSV). But it stands on its own and has nothing to do with warlike apocalyptic. The "crown of life" or a similar phrase appears several places in the New Testament and is not always to be understood as a military image.

6. The texts are assembled in the appendix and will only be partially repeated here in translation. [Harnack's collection of texts in the original languages is omitted here.]

7. "Finally, be strong in the Lord and in the strength of his might. Put on the whole armor of God, that you may be able to stand against the wiles of the devil. For we are not contending against flesh and blood, but against the principalities, against the powers, against the world rulers of this present darkness, against the spiritual hosts of wickedness in the heavenly places. Therefore take the whole armor of God, that you may be able

virtually everything, the weaponry and the battle, is meant in a spiritual sense. It states expressly that it is concerned with the "gospel of peace." So the whole presentation is given the character of a lofty paradox, and the military element is essentially neutralized.

One aspect of this passage may not be neutralized or understood allegorically: there is a real warfare going on. The apostle is deeply convinced that each Christian must be a warrior and must endure fearful though certainly victorious battles. There are battles against flesh and blood, but those are the lesser ones, or rather their significance disappears when compared with the battles against the powers of the demons. As the "world rulers of this present darkness" and, still worse, as "the spiritual hosts of wickedness in the heavenly places" (RSV), they besiege and attack the Christians constantly. Only an unrelieved warfare carried out with all the powers of the good and the holy will be able to defend against them.[8]

This notion of the apostle has had an immense effect: the Christian life is a battle with the demons! It is hard to say whether this concept inspired in the Christians of the next generations more in the way of strength or fear and dread; it is certain, however, that the concept never disappeared. It became a fixed form of their outlook on the world and of their spiritual discipline. It was to be of the highest importance in the history of ethics and the moral life that they

---

to withstand in the evil day, and having done all, to stand. Stand therefore, having girded your loins with truth, and having put on the breastplate of righteousness, and having shod your feet with the equipment of the gospel of peace; besides all these, taking the shield of faith, with which you can quench all the flaming darts of the evil one. And take the helmet of salvation, and the sword of the Spirit. . . . with all prayer and supplication" (RSV).

8. We do not find this in the moral admonitions of the Old Testament insofar as they speak of a battle. Demonology first developed in Judaism through external influences in the intertestamental period.

transferred the inner fight to an external one and put demons in place of flesh and blood and in place of selfishness. We cannot pursue this side of the matter further here, but we will encounter it frequently in what follows.

In spite of his instruction that every Christian must participate in this battle, Paul did not describe Christians generally as soldiers. Yet he certainly did characterize himself and his co-workers in this way. And this characterization is not a passing thing but remains constant: the apostle and missionary is a soldier. He calls his co-workers "my fellow soldiers" (Philem. 2; Phil. 2:25 RSV). Whoever has been in prison with him has been a "prisoner of war"[9] (Rom. 16:7; Col. 4:10; Philem. 23). The apostle can require support for his living from the congregations, for "Who serves as a soldier at his own expense?" (1 Cor. 9:7 RSV). Paul writes to the Corinthians who have slanderously reproached him, "I robbed other churches by accepting support from them in order to serve you" (2 Cor. 11:8 RSV). In a series of splendid images he had previously displayed to them his deeds of war (2 Cor. 10:3–6 RSV): "For though we live in the world we are not carrying on a worldly war, for the weapons of our warfare are not worldly but have divine power to destroy strongholds. We destroy arguments and every proud obstacle to the knowledge of God, and take every thought captive to obey Christ, being ready to punish every disobedience, when your obedience is complete." Thus speaks one who is used to understanding himself as a warrior and regarding his work as a campaign.

What is materially most significant in all of these images is that the military analogy is capable of proving that the missionary is entitled to receive his living from the congregations which he has established. In this way the image is made into a proof, and the approximation to the warrior is

---

9. [RSV reads "fellow prisoners."]

no longer simply on the ideal plane. In the years which followed, this Pauline military axiom was always retained, and it developed into a right within the law of the church.

The composer of the pastoral Epistles imitated Paul (or does Paul speak in these passages himself?) when he charged Timothy (1 Tim. 1:18) to wage the good warfare and admonished him (2 Tim. 2:3) that he should take his share of suffering as a good soldier of Christ Jesus (both times "good" renders καλός). Here we have for the first time the plain formula *miles Christi,* although even here it does not apply to each Christian, but only to the missionary and leader of the congregation. The passage has become important in still another respect. The writer continues: "No soldier on service gets entangled in civilian pursuits, since his aim is to satisfy the one who enlisted him. An athlete is not crowned unless he competes according to the rules."[10] Here we have a second military image, which is put forward as an analogy and also as a proof: the Christian missionary, like the soldier, should keep himself free from all civilian pursuits. He should have his own course of life, which is determined by his calling alone, separated from the way of life, the duties, and the cares of the civilians. This axiom, which finds expression here for the first time and is grounded in the military, had an extraordinarily rich development in the following period. It did not create the order of clergy in distinction from the laity, but gave it the tightest hold. It also affected in a decisive way the formation of monasticism. It is one of the powerful maxims whose observance penetrated the entire fellowship and changed its character. Above the Catholic priesthood and above the Catholic orders of monks in all the centuries

---

10. [So RSV. Harnack has: "Niemand, der zu Felde zieht, verflicht sich mit den Geschäften des (bürgerlichen) Lebens, damit er dem Feldherrn gefalle; wer aber kämpft, wird nur gekrönt, wenn er der Anordnung gemäss (νομίμως) kämpft."]

stand the words "No soldier entangles himself in civilian pursuits." They have often enough become a declaration of war. Above all else, however, they have caused the "civilian" (*bürgerlichen*) life and the "civilian" calling to appear to be of inferior value, because it says in our passage that the military commander, that is, God, looks with pleasure on those who free themselves from worldly pursuits. So arose the theme for a mighty fugue in world history, but its tones were often neither melodious nor peaceful. However, in the beginning, the principle was completely necessary and wholesome.

Here we have two military axioms which were accepted in earliest Christianity: the Christian missionary and teacher gets his living from others and does not involve himself in "civilian" pursuits. They are polar in their effect and therefore imply a whole class structure.

Another not unimportant feature is to be found in the passage from 2 Timothy. Only that warrior will be crowned who fights according to the regulations (νομίμως). If the reference here is perhaps to an athlete, still the close connection with what comes before shows that for the writer the thought of battle is paramount. The battle of the Christian teacher, just like that of the military fighter, is only worthwhile if it is carried out in a disciplined way, that is, according to the regulations of the commander. Military discipline first emerges here as an analogy for the manner of the Christian's warfare. This conception too would have a rich history in time to come.

We find in the earliest Christian writings all of the following: the soldier, weapons of various kinds, wages (cf. the serious word of Rom. 6:23, "The wages of sin is death"), discipline, the wreath, gifts *(donativa),* imprisonment, pillage, fortification, bulwark, military onslaughts, and the heretics, who like cunning foes sneak into the houses and take away the women as captives (2 Tim. 3:6). But more significant is the firm conception that the Christian teacher is *miles Christi,*

39

who may require his living from others and does not involve himself in "civilian" pursuits.

It is certainly no accident that we find the following statements in the First Letter of Clement (ca. A.D. 96), which is the most ancient writing we possess from the Roman church: "We should not be deserters from his will" (chap. 21); "What world will receive any one of the deserters from him?" (chap. 28).[11]

We also find the following (chap. 37): "Let us then, men and brethren, with all energy act the part of soldiers, in accordance with His holy commandments. Let us consider those who serve under our generals, with what order, obedience, and submissiveness they perform the things which are commanded them. All are not prefects, nor commanders of a thousand, nor of a hundred, nor of fifty, nor the like, but each one in his own rank performs the things commanded by the king and the generals."[12]

The Roman Clement not only regarded all Christians as warriors of God, but he looked with satisfaction and pride on the Roman military and regarded the obedience and the ordered ranks of the army as patterns for the Christian congregation.

It is like a prediction of the future that this early Roman presbyter praises the military obedience of Christians as the right relationship not only toward God but also toward the ecclesiastical authorities, and that he sets forth the distinction between those who command and those who obey in the church as being just as essential as it is in the army. Paul had

---

11. [*ANF* 1:11 reads, "we should not leave the post which His will has assigned us." *ANF* 1:12 reads, "Or what world will receive any of those who run away from Him?"] We also find this admonition in the Pseudo-Clementine *Letter to James,* chap. 17 and chap. 11. Cf. also Pseudo-Clement, *Homil.* XI, 16 (the word in question is λειποτάκτειν, λειποτάκτης).

12. [*ANF* 1:15.]

once used the ancient image of the different parts of the body in order to correct the pride of the Corinthians with regard to spiritual gifts; Clement wants to reduce the independence and freedom of individual members compared to the ecclesiastical officeholders. It is on this account that he presents the military organization as a model for Christians, because a strict line is drawn there between the officers and the soldiers: the former command, the latter obey. The military analogy benefits the clergy here. All Christians are soldiers, but just for this reason they have to obey their commanders, the presbyters.

Paul certainly did not write in this way. The step which is indicated in this letter of Clement is a great one. There must be officers in the church, and strict obedience to them will be required, because Christians are God's soldiers.

In the literature of the century which follows, military images are not found in abundance, but they do occur. In a manner similar to Paul in Ephesians 6, Ignatius presents a detailed military image (*To Polycarp* 6): "Please ye Him under whom ye fight, and from whom ye receive your wages ($\tau\grave{\alpha}$ $\grave{o}\psi\acute{\omega}\nu\iota\alpha$). Let none of you be found a deserter ($\delta\epsilon\sigma\acute{\epsilon}\rho\tau\omega\rho$). Let your baptism endure as your arms ($\acute{o}\pi\lambda\alpha$); your faith as your helmet; your love as your spear; your patience as a complete panoply ($\pi\alpha\nu o\pi\lambda\acute{\iota}\alpha$). Let your works be the charge assigned to you ($\delta\epsilon\pi\acute{o}\sigma\iota\tau\alpha$), that ye may receive a worthy recompense ($\tau\grave{\alpha}$ $\acute{\alpha}\kappa\kappa\epsilon\pi\tau\alpha$)."[13] Here Ignatius, like Clement, regards all Christians as soldiers of God. The Latin military technical terms which he has interspersed in his admonition, composed in Greek, are to be explained by the fact that he was writing while being transported; he heard these words frequently from the soldiers who were accompanying him. So it is that words like $\delta\epsilon\sigma\acute{\epsilon}\rho\tau\omega\rho$ = *desertor*, $\delta\epsilon\pi\acute{o}\sigma\iota\tau\alpha$ = *deposita*, $\acute{\alpha}\kappa\kappa\epsilon\pi\tau\alpha$ = *accepta* are found in an edifying letter

---

13. [*ANF* 1:95.]

written in Greek.[14] Apparently Ignatius used a military image in one other place (*To the Smyrnaeans* 1). He speaks of the "standard" (σύσσημον) that Jesus has lifted up through his resurrection. He means the cross as a standard "for the faithful, whether among Jews or Gentiles."[15] The cross as *vexillum Christi,* as banner and standard, became a very beloved image in subsequent years. The Latin hymn "Vexilla regis prodeunt" is famous.

Passing over what is of lesser significance, I turn now to Justin (ca. 150), the authoritative apologist of the second century. In his *Apology* (I, 11) he informs the emperor that the Christians are not looking forward to an earthly kingdom and that the heavenly kingdom which is coming soon is to be a kingdom of peace (I, 39). The prophecy of Isaiah 2 is of special worth to Justin (RSV):

> For out of Zion shall go forth the law,
>   and the word of the Lord from Jerusalem.
> He shall judge between the nations,
>   and shall decide for many peoples;
> and they shall beat their swords into plowshares,
>   and their spears into pruning hooks;
> nation shall not lift up sword against nation,
>   neither shall they learn war any more.

Justin seeks to show the emperor that this prediction has

---

14. Two hundred years later a Latin military word even appears in the canons of Nicaea. Canon 12: ". . . by means of gifts (βενεφικίοις, *beneficiis*) have acquired again their military station." Concerning the penetration of military words into the language of the rabbis in the time of the Roman Empire, see Emil Schürer, *Geschichte des jüdischen Volkes im Zeitalter Jesu Christi,* Bd. 2³, p. 44. [4th ed., 3 vols. with index (Leipzig: Hinrichs, 1901–11); Eng. trans. *A History of the Jewish People in the Time of Jesus Christ,* 5 vols., trans. John Macpherson et al. (Edinburgh: T. & T. Clark, 1897–98); vol. 1 (newly translated) rev. and ed. Geza Vermes and Fergus Millar (Edinburgh: T. & T. Clark, 1973).]

15. [*ANF* 1:86.]

begun to be fulfilled in the Christian mission.[16] For "we do not wage war against our enemies," rather we go cheerfully to our deaths for the good. Christians are warriors of a special kind, peaceful warriors. Yet when it comes to loyalty to their cause and courage to die they excel everyone: "But if the soldiers enrolled by you, and who have taken the military oath, prefer their allegiance to their own life, and parents, and country, and all kindred, though you can offer them nothing incorruptible, it were verily ridiculous if we, who earnestly long for incorruption, should not endure all things, in order to obtain what we desire from Him who is able to grant it."[17]

Although prior to the year 180 the notion that Christians are warriors is attested to in many ways, one is still surprised to find that the name "soldiers of Christ" appears as a technical designation for Christians in the novellike work "Acts of Paul" written about this time. The cupbearer of Nero, who has been converted by Paul, declares that Christ is the king of the ages and will destroy all kingdoms. To this Nero responds:

"Patroclus, dost thou also serve in that king's army?" He confesses it, and still other Christians who are standing before the Emperor speak: "We are also in the army of that king of the

---

16. Some decades later another apologist, Melito, developed this concept in such a way as to bring together the peace for which flatterers gave credit to the empire with the peace which was brought by Christ. According to the working of divine Providence, Augustus and Jesus appeared at the same time, and since then there has been a reign of peace. (See Melito in Eusebius, *History of the Christian Church* IV, 22.) Justin knew nothing of such courtly falsifications of history. Hippolytus presents us with the exact opposite of Melito's view of history. In his *Commentary on Daniel* (IV, 9, 2–3) he explains that the universal rule of Augustus is a demonic imitation of the kingdom of Christ. The taxation under Augustus was no accident, but rather an intentional divine dispensation: it should now appear who was a Roman and who was a Christian.

17. [*Apology* I, 39; *ANF* 1:176.]

ages . . ." and (Nero) commanded that the soldiers of the great king be sought out, and he issued a decree to this effect, that all who were found to be Christians and soldiers of Christ should be put to death. Now Paul is also brought before Nero. Nero addresses him: "Man of the great king, but (now) my prisoner, why did it seem good to thee to come secretly into the empire of the Romans and enlist soldiers from my province?" Paul: "Caesar, not only from thy province do we enlist soldiers, but from the whole world. For this charge has been laid upon us, that no man be excluded who wishes to serve my king. If thou also think it good, do him service! . . . For we do not march, as you suppose, with a king who comes from the earth, but one from heaven . . . I am no deserter from Christ, but a lawful soldier of the living God."[18]

One could almost describe this language as seditious in spite of the declaration that Christ is no earthly king. It is, of course, in a novel, a quite unreliable story, that we find these words, but that does nothing to the case. The author of this "history," a presbyter of Asia Minor, perceives that whoever becomes a Christian thereby ceases to be a Roman. Christ, the heavenly king, is contrasted with the earthly king, and Christians are exclusively soldiers of this heavenly king.[19]

One may not assume that this was the ruling sentiment among Christians. The novelist uses heavy brushstrokes because he is writing about the apostolic age. This was a heroic age in the eyes of Christians at that time, and on this account the heroes were allowed to speak more bravely and reck-

---

18. [Edgar Hennecke, *New Testament Apocrypha*, 2 vols., ed. Wilhelm Schneemelcher, trans. R. McL. Wilson (London, 1965; Philadelphia: Westminster Press, 1963–65), 2:384–86.]

19. Cf. also *Acta Petri cum Simone* 7, where Peter says, "You men, who are soldiers in relationship to Christ, who hope in Christ!" [The Latin version (Lipsius) contains no reference to soldiers, nor do the standard English translations (see Hennecke, 2:301). But Harnack presents an original Greek text in his appendix to *Militia Christi* (p. 96 in the Darmstadt edition, not included here) which does.]

lessly than one would speak oneself. But we can gather from the words of this legend that Christians understood themselves to be soldiers of Christ.

As would be expected, military images, apart from the purely rhetorical, are lacking for the most part in the Christian philosopher Clement of Alexandria (ca. 200). Therefore only a few samples of that rhetoric will be set forth. In *Excerpta ex Theodoto* 85 he uses a military image suggested by Paul (Ephesians 6) and speaks of being armed with the weapons of the Lord (τὰ κυριακὰ ὅπλα). There is likewise a recollection of Ephesians 6 when he writes in the *Exhortation to the Heathen* (XI, 116):

> The loud trumpet, when sounded, collects the soldiers, and proclaims war. And shall not Christ, breathing a strain of peace to the ends of the earth, gather together his own soldiers, the soldiers of peace? Well, by His blood and by the word, He has gathered the bloodless host of peace and assigned to them the kingdom of heaven. The trumpet of Christ is His Gospel. He has blown it and we have heard. "Let us array ourselves in the armor of peace, putting on the breastplate of righteousness, and taking the shield of faith, etc." So the Apostle in the spirit of peace commands. These are our invulnerable weapons; armed with these, let us face the evil one; "the fiery darts of the evil one" let us quench with the sword-points dipped in water, that have been baptized by the Word, etc.[20]

In *The Stromata* (VII, 16, 100) he says, "As then, in war the soldier must not leave the post which the commander has assigned him, so neither must we desert the post assigned by the Word, whom we have received as the guide of knowledge and of life."[21] *The Instructor* (I, 7, 54): "As therefore the general directs the phalanx, consulting the safety of his sol-

---

20. [*ANF* 2:204.]
21. [*ANF* 2:552.]

diers . . . so also the Instructor guides the children to a saving course of conduct."[22] In the treatise *Who Is the Rich Man That Shall Be Saved?* (chap. 25) he speaks in deeply felt words about the battle within, which is more difficult than any exterior war or persecution and only ends with death: "For he carries the enemy about everywhere in himself."[23] But apart from this picture of the inner conflict, warlike images are far from his thoughts; in fact, he renounces them. In the same treatise about the rich man, he writes (chap. 34), "Collect for thyself an unarmed, an unwarlike, a bloodless, a passionless, a stainless host."[24] He means the widows, orphans, and needy, and he says that these through their prayers and petitions, like soldiers commanded by God, will protect the rich who are benevolent. "For it is not in war," he says in *The Instructor* (I, 12, 98–99), "but in peace, that we are trained. War needs great preparation . . . but peace and love, simple and quiet sisters, require no arms nor excessive preparation."[25]

At the time of Clement there had already existed within Christianity for several decades an active and widespread movement which declared itself against the Old Testament and rejected the God of Israel because he was warlike and thereby contradicted the gospel. In the church of Marcion, the most remarkable reformer of the second century, it was professed that the God of the Old Testament could not possibly be the Father of Jesus Christ. The one was gracious, compassionate, brought peace and forbade striving and war, while the other was warlike, inexorable, and cruel. Marcion demonstrated in a series of antitheses based on the Old Tes-

---

22. [*ANF* 2:223.]
23. [*ANF* 2:598.]
24. [*ANF* 2:601.]
25. [*ANF* 2:234–35.]

tament and the Gospel how different were the Jewish God and Jesus Christ. In these antitheses the opposition of the acts of war of the Jewish God to the gentleness of Jesus played a major part. The fathers of the church who combated Marcion found themselves placed in the uncomfortable position of either having to defend the Old Testament warrior God as such or to conceive of the war stories allegorically. In addition to this, and against their own inclination and conviction, they had to look for sayings and stories in the New Testament in which Christ and the Father whom he proclaimed also appeared to be warlike, in order to produce an agreement. Marcion undoubtedly understood the Christian concept of God in an essentially correct way. The idea of a development of the Jewish God-concept into the Christian one was, of course, as far removed from him as it was from his opponents; so he had to break with the antecedents of Christianity, and his Catholic opponents had to falsify the Christian concept of God with antiquated notions. Both erred, for no other solutions were possible. It will always be to the glory of the Marcionite church, however, that it would rather cast away the Old Testament than tarnish the image of the Father of Jesus Christ by mixing in traces of a warlike God.

The most renowned opponent of the Gnostics and of Marcion in the Greek church, and the greatest theologian of his age, was Origen (first half of the third century). He too, like Clement, had a thoroughly peaceable nature as a Christian and as a philosopher. He would most certainly have preferred to throw overboard anything that was martial. But the letter of Holy Scripture did not allow that, and Origen was a convinced scriptural theologian. It is instructive to see how he came to terms with war. First, he allegorized the holy wars related in the books of the Old Testament in a most thoroughgoing way. (See especially his commentaries on

Numbers and on Joshua.) The heretics who take offense at these wars misunderstand them. What is meant are the battles against sin and the powers of darkness. Joshua, in the dim past, had presented a model of the great battle which Jesus and the Christians would wage against these powers. So there is no warlike God even in the Old Testament. (See *Hom. in Jesu Nave* 11 fin. 12 init., ed. Lommatzsch.) "If the horrible wars related in the Old Testament were not to be interpreted in a spiritual sense, the apostles would never have transmitted the Jewish history books for reading in the church to the disciples of Christ, who came to teach peace" (*Hom. in Jesu Nave* 15 t. 11, p. 130).[26] Hence, the Old Testament is a holy document for Christians if one interprets it spiritually; in many places the literal meaning is not normative, but objectionable. Origen then proceeds to state in an unequivocally clear way that the Apostle Paul taught that Christians may no longer conduct "fleshly" wars but only spiritual ones: "He gives orders to the soldiers of Christ just like a military commander" (Ephesians 6 follows), and "If we serve in the correct way as soldiers under Joshua's (Jesus') direction, we must root out the vices in ourselves."

Because of Ephesians 6 and other passages, Origen is required to allow for the spiritual warfare of Christians. So we find the designation *milites Christi* in his works as well. (See *De principiis* III, 2, 5, among many other passages.) "Jesus encourages his soldiers with the words 'Be of good cheer, I have overcome the world'" (*Hom. in Jesu Nave* 7 t. 11, p. 65). Because of the Old Testament the expression "camp of the Lord" *(castra domini)* for the church was unavoidable, and Origen used it (for example, *Hom. in Jesu Nave* 7 t. 11, p. 67). Just so, he speaks of the Christian military oath, the

---

26. [All quotations from Origen's homilies on Joshua *(Jesu Nave)*, Numbers, and so forth are from Harnack's ·German, since no English translation is available.]

sacramentum militiae (*Hom. in Jesu Nave* 4 t. 11, pp. 46–47).[27] However, as Origen now considered Ephesians 6 more closely, and the passage in the Letter of Timothy about soldiers of Christ who do not entangle themselves in civilian pursuits, he came to some remarkable conclusions. The congregations in his day had already become very worldly, and the greater number of Christians were lukewarm and weak. Origen was too honest to say that they were all "warriors of Christ," fighting a life-and-death battle with the demons who ruled the world. But he could not find a way out by saying the clergy were the soldiers of Christ, because in that order as well there were too many halfhearted Christians. Who then are the real warriors of Christ? Origen turned around the teaching in 2 Timothy and said that the real soldiers are those who do not entangle themselves in civilian pursuits, hence the ascetics. Origen became the father of the concept in the Catholic churches that the ascetic (the monk would soon follow him) was the real Christian combatant. He carries on an incessant battle against sin. He even sees the demons and overcomes them in fierce struggle. He and he alone is the soldier whom Paul depicts in the Letter to the Ephesians. These soldiers fight too "for the rest of the people," for the great number of weak ones of all sorts. They themselves are always small in number: "How few there are in the church who endeavor to fight for the truth!" But the host of Gideon was small and still won the victory. The weapons of these warriors are prayers and fasts, meditations and good works, justice and piety, meekness, chastity, and abstinence. In their battle against the demons they will be sup-

---

27. Cf. also *Hom. in Iudic.* 6 (t. 11, p. 258): "Before we learn the (spiritual) conduct of war, before we are able to plan the battles of the Lord, we will be protected by the angels, the princes; after we have tasted the sacraments of the heavenly military service (*sacramenta militiae caelestis*) and have strengthened ourselves with the bread of life, we will be awakened by the apostolic trumpet to the battles." (Ephesians 6 follows.)

ported by the prayers of the just who have departed this life. "But the rest of the Christian people also receive something from the spoils of victory, if they stay in the camp of peace, if they stand still and do not fall away from Moses, but remain in the law of God." The battles of these warriors of God are also directed against the heretics.[28] They fight "for the church" against the enemies of the truth. The enemies of truth are those who lead men astray into disputing the teachings of the church or giving themselves over to the sensual life of pleasure. The fighters are "heroes"; the choir of angels looks down on them, and a glorious reward awaits them. The others, however, who do not lead an ascetic life are certainly "men," but not heroes. Foremost among the heroes of Christ are Paul and Peter, "who fought so much, who conquered so many barbaric peoples, laid low so many enemies, won so much spoil, celebrated so many triumphs, who return with bloody hands from the massacre of the enemy, whose feet are bathed in blood and whose hands are washed in the blood of sinners; for they have defeated and killed whole battalions of the most diverse demons; for if they had not defeated them, they could not have captured prisoners, namely the whole company of those who now believe in Christ. The one who snatches men away from the domination of the demons, of him it can be said that he has won a bloody victory over the demons" (*Hom. in Num.* 25 t. 10, pp. 310ff.). "The weaker and not yet perfect ones fight only against flesh and blood, the perfect, however, against the evil spirits under heaven" (*Hom. in Jesu Nave* 11 t. 11, p. 110).

---

28. Cf. *Hom. in Jesu Nave* 18 (t. 11, p. 160): "The cities and walls which we must tear down are the dogmas of the godless and the syllogisms of the philosophers, who set up ungodly teachings opposed to the law of God, as they cherish the heathens and barbarians. However, one must also understand the false explanations of Scripture of the heretics as being the high towering forts which they erect as upon high mountains." *Hom. in Iudic.* 8 (t. 11, p. 269): the heretics are Midianites.

Those are the notes of the Middle Ages which Origen has already sounded. What a rich history this concept has had: ascetics and monks are the real soldiers of Christ who lead the battles of the Lord! In another passage (*Hom. in Num.* 26 t. 10, pp. 316ff.) Origen divides the "soldiers" into officers and common soldiers and divides the noncombatants into those who are permanently and those who are temporarily in that status. The officers are the strong ascetics who meditate on the law of God day and night. There is no discord or strife among them. It can be said of them alone and not of all believers that they are of one mind and one soul, that they have everything in common, and that they offer what they have, their thoughts and works, to God.

If Jesus equals Joshua, then it follows that Jesus is "the prince of the military forces of the Lord," "for the whole heavenly militia, the angels, archangels, and so forth perform their service under his direction" (*Hom. in Jesu Nave* 6 t. 11, p. 59). The persecutions too which Christians endure here on earth, as well as their victories, stand under the military leadership of Jesus: "The kings of the earth, the Roman senate and the people and the nobility have banded together in order to vanquish at once the name of Jesus and of Israel, for they have established in their laws that there shall be no Christians. But under the leadership of Jesus his soldiers will always triumph, so that we too say as it is written in Ezra, 'From you, Lord, is the victory, and I am your servant'" (*Hom. in Jesu Nave* 9 t. 11, p. 100). "Also today," he writes (*Hom. in Iudic.* 9 t. 11, pp. 278ff.), "the prince of our army, our Lord and Savior Jesus Christ, calls to his soldiers and says, 'If anyone is fearful and anxious, he may not take part in my war.' In the words, 'He who does not hate his father' and so forth (one thinks here of the military oath—Harnack), Christ quite clearly excludes the fearful from his camp." Origen's heartfelt sigh in response to Eph. 4:8 is remarkably subjective (*Hom. in Num.* 18 t. 10, p. 227): "O that Christ

51

Jesus would always have me as a prisoner of war and carry me off as his spoil and that I might remain bound in his bands, so that I too deserved the name 'prisoner of Jesus Christ' as Paul boasted himself to be." Finally, he writes, "We establish two kinds of armed soldiers, the soldiers of God and the soldiers of the devil; and if the soldier of God wears the armor of righteousness, then undoubtedly the soldier of the devil wears the armor of unrighteousness" (*Select. in Psalm* t. 12, pp. 178–79).

But Origen wants to know nothing about worldly military service; he regards it as forbidden. "And none fight better for the king than we do," he writes (*Against Celsus* VIII, 73). "We do not indeed fight under him, although he require it; but we fight on his behalf, forming a special army—an army of piety—by offering our prayers to God."[29] (For particulars about this, see the second chapter.)

The *militia Christi* concept finds expression in the Latin church of the West in a way that is rhetorically weaker but stronger in substance. We find this in Tertullian. (He was, we should remember, the son of a centurion in the army.) He is opposed to the secular military profession (this will be discussed later), but the concept of spiritual warfare is frequent and appears to be necessary in his works. He characterizes all Christians as *milites Christi* in many passages,[30] with special reference to the martyrs in several of them. The courtroom and the prison are the places of battle in which the great contest with the devil is fought out.[31] We first find

---

29. [*ANF* 4:668.]

30. See, for example, *Ad Martyras* 3: "Yet we were called to the warfare of the living God (at baptism—Harnack)" [ANF 3:694].

31. *Ad Martyras* 1: "The prison, indeed, is the devil's house as well, wherein he keeps his family. But you have come within its walls for the very purpose of trampling the wicked one under foot in his chosen abode" [ANF 3:693].

the name *imperator* (commander) used for Christ in Tertullian's writings.[32] For him, the bishops, presbyters, and deacons are the officers *(duces)*, the laity are the enlisted men *(gregarius numerus)*.[33] Military discipline and the privations and exertions of soldiers are required of Christians.[34] The heretics are the rebels and deserters from the church.[35]

What gave the military images a special hold in the churches of the West was the concept *sacramentum*. Exhaus-

---

32. *On Exhortation to Chastity* 12: "For are not we, too, soldiers? Soldiers, indeed, subject to all the stricter discipline, that we are subject to so great a General *(imperator)*" [*ANF* 4:56]. *De Fuga in Persecutione* (hereafter, *De Fuga*) 10: "A worthy soldier he furnishes to his commander *(imperator)* Christ, who, so amply armed by the apostle, as soon as he hears persecution's trumpet, runs off from the day of persecution!" [*ANF* 4:121].

33. *De Fuga* 11: "Thus, too, with the leaders (the clergy—Harnack) turning their backs, who of the common rank will hope to persuade men to stand firm in the battle?" [*ANF* 4:122].

34. *Ad Martyras* 3: "Well, no soldier comes out to the campaign laden with luxuries, nor does he go to action from his comfortable chamber, but from the light and narrow tent, where every kind of hardness, roughness and unpleasantness must be put up with. Even in peace soldiers inure themselves to war by toils and inconveniences—marching in arms, running over the plain, working at the ditch, making the *testudo* (a formation in close ranks with shields held high—Harnack), engaging in many arduous labors. The sweat of the brow is on everything, that bodies and minds may not shirk at having to pass from shade to sunshine, from sunshine to icy cold, from the robe of peace to the coat of mail, from silence to clamor, from quiet to tumult. In like manner, O blessed ones, count whatever is hard in this lot of yours as a discipline of your powers of mind and body" [*ANF* 3:694].

Apology 50: "Well, it is quite true that it is our desire to suffer, but it is in the way that the soldier longs for war. No one indeed suffers willingly, since suffering necessarily implies fear and danger. Yet the man who objected to the conflict, both fights with all his strength, and when victorious, he rejoices in the battle, because he reaps from it glory and spoil. It is our battle to be summoned to your tribunals that there, under fear of execution, we may battle for the truth. But the day is won when the object of the struggle is gained. This victory of ours gives us the glory of pleasing God, and the spoil of life eternal" [*ANF* 3:54].

35. *The Prescription Against Heretics* 41: "Nowhere is promotion easier than in the camp of rebels (that is, heretics—Harnack), where the mere fact of being there is a foremost service" [*ANF* 3:263].

tive research into this word, which is found so frequently as early as Tertullian, proves that *sacramentum* had a double meaning in the language of the Latin church from the beginning. First, it meant a visible sign for a spiritual reality, which stands in a mysterious union with the reality itself. Second, it meant the military oath of allegiance. That it was received in the Western church with this meaning is quite remarkable. Along with other military technical terms *(statio, vexillum, donativa)* which were taken up into the language of the Latin Bible and the Latin church, it seems to indicate that the military element was at times very strong in some of the earliest Latin congregations. Tertullian does not introduce the concept *sacramentum* = military oath as something unknown. He writes in *Ad Martyras* 3: "We were called to the army of the living God even as we repeated the words of the oath *(sacramentum)* (namely, at baptism—Harnack)."[36] *The Prescription Against Heretics* 20: "In this way all are primitive and all are apostolic, whilst they are all proved to be one, in (unbroken) unity, by their peaceful communion, and title of brotherhood, and bond of hospitality *(contesseratio hospitalitatis)*—privileges which no other rule directs than the one tradition of the selfsame sacrament (namely, the confession of faith made at baptism—Harnack)."[37] *The Chaplet,* or *De Corona* (hereafter, *De Corona*), 11: "Do we believe it lawful for a human oath *(sacramentum)* to be superadded to one divine (at baptism—Harnack), for a man to come under promise to another master after Christ, and to abjure father, mother, and all nearest kinfolk (a play on the wording of the military oath—Harnack)?"[38] *On Idolatry* 19: "There is no agreement between the divine and the human sacrament, the standard of Christ and the standard of the devil, the camp of

---

36. [So Harnack. ANF 3:694 has "yet we were called to the warfare of the living God in our very response to the sacramental words."]
37. [*ANF* 3:252, altered.]
38. [*ANF* 3:99.]

light and the camp of darkness."[39] *Scorpiace* 4: "I am . . . bid (to) love (God) with my whole being, that I may die for Him. Serving as a soldier under this oath *(sacramentum)*, I am challenged by the enemy. . . . In maintaining this oath, I fight furiously in battle, am wounded, hewn to pieces, slain. Who wished this fatal issue to his soldier, but he who sealed him by such an oath?"[40]

One can no longer speak here of a mere image. Tertullian and the Latin Christians with him regard themselves as real soldiers of Christ. At baptism they swore the oath to him, they promised themselves to Christ, and now they are in duty bound to him and only to him as his warriors.[41] Hence, they like to use military speech and expressions. The early Roman Christian Hermas said, "I stand guard,"[42] and meant by that solemn fasting. We see in Tertullian that *statio* = "fast"[43] had become a quite common expression, scarcely an

---

39. [*ANF* 3:73.]

40. [*ANF* 3:637.] See also *The Shows* 24: "When you go over to the enemy's camp, you throw down your arms, desert the standards and the oaths of allegiance *(sacramenta)* to your chief" [*ANF* 3:89, altered].

41. The name giving (*nomen dare*, ἀπογράφεσθαι) before baptism and at the induction into the army also constitutes a contact point. Whether the Christian custom of receiving a new name at baptism is in any way connected with the similar military practice is questionable. However, after the custom had become more frequent in the church (fourth century) there arose here in the consciousness a further parallel between the soldier's profession and the Christian's profession. The practice of taking a new surname became ever more widespread in the whole empire in the third and fourth centuries. The reasons for this are not yet completely understood. For the soldiers there are special considerations: they wanted to separate themselves from civilians by means of the chosen names; also the increasing multiplicity of languages in the army and the great number of barbarian names made it advisable to take a new Latin name. The Christians were also motivated by wanting to distinguish themselves by name from non-Christians. Investigations into these questions, in which even Mommsen interested himself in his last years, are still in their beginning stages and are scattered. See, for example, Höfling, *Das Sakrament der Taufe* I (1846), pp. 369ff., and my *Mission und Ausbreitung*, pp. 304ff. [*Mission and Expansion*, 1:422ff.].

42. *Simil.* V, 1: στατίωνα ἔχω.

43. In the sense of "fixed and solemn fasts."

image anymore, but rather a Christian military function.[44] In the writing *On Prayer* 19, he emphasizes the military origin of the word himself: "If the 'station' has received its name from the example of military life—for we withal are God's military—of course no gladness or sadness chancing to the camp abolishes the 'stations' of the soldiers."[45] It is similar with the other expressions like *vexilla,*[46] *signa,* and so forth. It is most interesting that militarism also penetrated the old Latin translation of the Bible.[47] The expression "my burden is light" (Matt. 11:30 RSV) appears in Tertullian (*On Monogamy* 2) and in Latin Bibles as "levem sarcinam domini" ("the light pack of the Lord"). Christ is thought of here as the captain who sets the weight of his soldiers' packs.[48] The words of Rom. 6:23, "The wages of sin is death, but the gift of God is life," appear in the Latin Bible as Tertullian read them: "stipendia delinquentiae mors, donativum autem dei vita" (". . . the donative of God is life").

Corssen writes:[49]

That is an excellent translation, which heightens the original. It proceeds from a very imaginative view of the context. The notion of the regular wages awakens the thought of the special gift of grace. The Lord of Hosts, set in parallel to the earthly warlord, pays with eternal life. Tertullian certainly found the translation at hand. Without being able to presuppose it, he could not say what he did about the Christian soldier who would not put on the wreath proffered to him as a reward for his bravery: "completely equipped in the apostle's armor and crowned more worthily with the white crown of martyrdom, he awaits in prison the *donative of Christ.*" On the basis of the Greek text no one could understand the allusion, but the

44. See *De Corona* 11; *On Fasting* 1, 10, 13; *De Fuga* 1; *To His Wife* II, 4.
45. [*ANF* 3:687.]
46. *Of Patience* 14; *De Corona* 11: here the military flags are expressly the rivals of the flag of Christ.
47. Corssen calls attention to this in *Zwei neue Fragmente der Weingartner Prophetenhandschrift* (1899), pp. 49–50.
48. Cf. *On Fasting* 12: The martyr in prison is to get rid of his baggage (*impedimenta*).
49. Corssen, pp. 49–50.

reader who was accustomed to the above translation of Romans would know immediately which word of the apostle the soldier in prison was depending upon.

The expression *donativum* appears elsewhere in the linguistic usage of Christians. "The Holy Ghost administers all *donativa* and dispenses them" (*Acts of the Martyrdom of Perpetua,* chap. 1). Tertullian renders Eph. 4:8 "dedit data filiis hominum, id est donativa" ("he gave gifts to the sons of men; that is, donatives"). Corssen points out Wisd. of Sol. 2:10 and Sirach [Ecclus.] 25:7, 27, where πρεσβύτης and πρεσβύτερος respectively are rendered with *veteranus,* and Wisd. of Sol. 8:9, where πρὸσ συμβίωσιν is translated *contubernium* ("messmate").

Even the expression "priest of God" was originally only an image, but gradually the image became a reality and a formal Catholic order of priests came into being. Members of the Latin church did not go that far with the term "soldier of God"; the religion of peace forbade that. But they did come close to the realistic view. It is thus that we can account for these two observations about Tertullian's works—first, that in one passage he plays with the idea that Christians could turn into open enemies of the Roman Empire; second, that he was attentive to the "soldiers" in the religion of Mithras.

He writes in *Apology* 37:

> If we desired, indeed, to act the part of open enemies, not merely of secret avengers, would there be any lacking of strength, whether of numbers or resources? Do the Moors, the Marcomanni, the Parthians themselves, or any single people, however great, inhabiting a distinct territory, and confined within its own boundaries, surpass in numbers one spread over all the world? . . . For what wars should we not be fit, not eager, even with unequal forces, we who so willingly yield ourselves to the sword, if in our religion it were not counted better to be slain than to slay?[50]

These words do not constitute a threat—he dared not

---

50. [*ANF* 3:45, altered.]

threaten!—but still they were an appeal to the uneasiness and fear of his enemies.

More interesting still is the relationship to the religion of Mithras.[51] In this religion, which had come from Persia, there really was a formal degree *(Grad)* of "soldier," and since the end of the second century, this religion was the one most widespread and beloved in the army. The third degree of seven was called *miles,* as Jerome relates.[52] On this step, which was the highest level of the catechumenate, one was enrolled in the holy army of the invincible god and fought under his command against the powers of evil.[53] Since the Christian religion had to contend with this religion especially—although this contention and the danger for Christianity have been overstated[54]—the fact that Mithraism also had a spiritual knighthood and sacraments must have been particularly irritating to the Christians. Nor was this the only correspondence between the two religions. Christians saw with revulsion that there were other things which were holy to them that also appeared in the religion of Mithras.[55] They could only explain this to themselves by saying that the devil was here aping the holy things and ordinances of the Christians. Tertullian writes in *Prescription Against Heretics* 40:

> It is the role of the devil to pervert the truth, and he, by the mystic rites of his idols, vies even with the essential portions of the sacraments of God. He too baptizes some—that is, his own believers and faithful followers; he promises the putting away of sins by a laver (of his own); and if my memory still

---

51. See Franz Cumont, *Les mystères de Mithra* (Brussels, 1900); Ger. trans. *Die Mysterien des Mithra,* trans. Gehrich (Leipzig, 1903). [Eng. trans. *Mysteries of Mithra,* 2d ed., trans. Thomas J. McCormack (1911; reprint ed., New York: Dover Publications, 1972).]

52. *Ep.* 107 *ad Laetam.*

53. Most Mithras worshipers remained on this step and were "soldiers" for life.

54. See my *Mission und Ausbreitung,* pp. 534ff. [*Mission and Expansion,* 2:317ff.]

55. In truth, the correspondences were external and accidental; they nowhere indicate a common root. An influence by the one religion on the other is at no point certain.

serves me (as the child of a soldier, Tertullian appears to have seen the ceremonies in the camp—Harnack), Mithras there (in the kingdom of Satan) sets his marks on the foreheads of his soldiers, celebrates also the oblation of bread, and introduces an image of a resurrection, and before a sword wreathes a crown.[56]

The final obscure saying is illuminated by another passage (*De Corona* 15). Many Christians who served in the army did not hesitate to accept the military wreath as an award, although, according to Tertullian, in doing so they tarnished themselves with idolatry.

> Blush, ye fellow-soldiers of his, henceforth not to be condemned even by him, but by some soldier of Mithras, who, at his initiation in the gloomy cavern, in the camp, it may well be said, of darkness, when at the sword's point a crown is presented to him, as though in mimicry of martyrdom, and thereupon put upon his head, is admonished to resist and cast it off, and if you like, transfer it to his shoulder, saying that Mithras is his crown. And thenceforth he is never crowned; and he has that for a mark to show who he is, if anywhere he be subjected to trial in respect of his religion; and he is at once believed to be a soldier of Mithras if he throws the crown away—if he says that in his god he has his crown. Let us take note of the devices of the devil, who is wont to ape some of God's things with no other design than, by the faithfulness of his servants, to put us to shame, and to condemn us.[57]

Although it is difficult to believe, it appears from this that the religious obligations of a follower of Mithras were respected in the army and that he was allowed a special exemption with regard to wearing that military decoration. How painful it must have been for the Christians that an exemption was granted to these men which was not accorded to them, thereby putting Christians in the position of having to transgress either military discipline or their faith!

In the century after Tertullian the sermons and exhorta-

---

56. [*ANF* 3:262, altered.]
57. [*ANF* 3:103.]

tions in the Western-Latin church are filled with images of military service, military discipline, and battle. One may flatly state that this schema and these images are the most frequent of all. Cyprian, whose tractates and letters were read more than Holy Scripture, adopted them fully. To assemble all the passages would be a pointless undertaking. It will suffice to become familiar with the main headings under which the concept of *militia Christi* (also *caelestis militia,* "heavenly militia") was expounded and applied.

1. Baptism remains the *sacramentum,* the military oath.[58]
2. Christ is the *imperator.*[59]
3. While all Christians are *milites,*[60] it is still the confessors and martyrs who are the real warriors, that is, the officers of God. They struggle with the demons and conquer them by their confession, their wounds, and their deaths.[61]
4. Their battle is a glorious warlike spectacle for God and is looked upon in admiration by him and the angels.[62] Chris-

---

58. See, for example, *Ep.* 10, 2: "sacrament and devotion of the soldier of God"; *Ep.* 54, 1; Arnobius, *Against the Heathen* II, 5: "to be unfaithful to Christ and cast off the sacraments of the army of salvation." Pseudo-Origen, *Tract. de libris ss. script.* 14 (p. 157): "sacrament of the army"; *Tract.* 18 (p. 198): "As soldiers of Christ, in these words of the sacraments we have taken an oath, we have been conscripted for this our contest." [Harnack's numbering of the epistles of Cyprian is identical with that in *The Fathers of the Church,* vol. 51 (Washington, D.C.: Catholic University of America Press, 1964). It does not coincide with *ANF.*]

59. See, for example, Cyprian, *Ep.* 15, 1; the Roman confessors in Cypr., *Ep.* 31, 4–5; Pseudo-Cyprian, *De mont. Sina et Sion* 8: "imperator et rex"; Commodian, *Instructions* II, 12: "imperium regis"; Lactantius, *Instit.* VI, 8: "magister et imperator omnium deus"; Lactant., VII, 27: "dominus et imperator." To my knowledge, Pope Damasus (fourth century) is the first to call the bishop's office *imperium;* to him a young cleric is a *tiro-miles* (recruit).

60. Commodian has a poem with the inscription "To the Soldiers of Christ" (*Instructions* II, 12). In the fourth century, the unknown author of the pseudo-Augustinian *Questions* writes, "We are soldiers of Christ and we receive our stipend and donative from him."

61. See, for example, Cypr., *Ep.* 10, 1–2; 15, 1; 28, 1–2 (here we have a special presentation of the military image); 46, 2; 54, 1; 76, 6; 77, 2.

62. See, for example, Cypr., Ep. 10, 2; 58, 4 ("Christ beholds his soldier"); 60, 2; 76, 4; Novatian, *De laude mart.* 26; Commodian, *Instruct.* II, 12.

tians do not fear the enemies, rather they provoke them.[63]
The coward is a deserter.[64]

5. The church (but also the prison) is the *castra dei*.[65]

6. The heretics, but above all the schismatics, are the rebels, and to them is due the punishment which befell Korah's rebellious band.[66]

7. The stations and vigils must be observed.[67]

8. One should flee the army of Mithras.[68]

A warlike mood, which was not morally harmless, had taken possession of third-century Latin Christianity. In the devotional literature of the West there appeared a tone which was fanatical and swaggering. The Christian threatened to become a *miles gloriosus* (a boastful soldier). Although the concern throughout was with spiritual warfare, there could also develop in this way earthly lust for battle and conflict, for spoils and victory in the common sense. Apart from fitful persecutions, the warlike language was in no way justified by the actual situation. It was an affectation. The Acts of the Martyrs which were written in the great persecution under Diocletian and his co-emperors, and even more, those which were written later, are often enough lacking in the calm and composure which were prescribed for Christians in their classic documents (putting the apocalyptic writings to one side). But who may criticize the bearing of people who had been signed over to the executioner and faced a frightening death?

---

63. The Roman confessors in Cyprian, *Ep.* 31, 4–5 and elsewhere.

64. Ibid.; Novatian in Cyprian, *Ep.* 30, 6; Lactant. *Instit.* VII, 27; Commodian, *Instruct.* II, 11 (a poem with the inscription "Deserters").

65. For example, Cypr. *Ep.* 10, 1; 46, 2; 54, 1; 58, 8; 60, 2; 61, 3; the Roman confessors in Cypr. *Ep.* 31, 4–5; Novatian in Cypr. *Ep.* 30, 6; Commodian, *Instruct.* II, 11.

66. For example, Cypr. *Ep.* 3, 3: 28, 2; 43, 5; 58, 10; 69, 8. In *Ep.* 59, 13, it states that the schismatics bear "parricidal arms" against the church.

67. For example, Lactant., *Instit.* VII, 27.

68. See Commodian in the poem "Deserters" (*Instruct.* II, 11): "Do not wander long as a soldier through caves of the wild beasts." [*ANF* 4:213, *The Instructions of Commodianus* 52.]

Their biographers alone are subject to our criticism.[69] They and the ascetic writers, if I see it correctly, are largely responsible for the shift in emphasis which occurred. Images of the battles against sin and evil desires (and the demons which cause them) diminished compared with images of the battles with demons as they were reputed to be at work in the persecutions by the heathen and the activities of the heretics. The earlier age was in this respect more concerned with the inner life. The "holy war" in the real sense of the word was, nevertheless, never preached in the pre-Constantinian period. And although individual confessors did give vent to seditious speech,[70] there is hardly a trace of uprisings or revolutions.[71] That is to the glory of the church as it still stood under the sword of the emperors! In some provinces the Christians were numerous and strong enough to band together and organize an uprising. They did not do it. It appears that it was only in the very earliest times that dangers had to be fought in this direction. That was when they were still deeply given over to apocalyptic and had not been fully freed from the Jewish political spirit (*jüdisch-politischen Geiste*). Those passages from the Gospels of Matthew and John cited earlier would not be understandable otherwise. At that time it must have been necessary to say expressly that the Kingdom of God is not of this world, that it is not to be defended by earthly weapons, that the Christian

---

69. After what has already been presented, we do not need to mention further that the Acts of the Martyrs, even the genuine ones, are full of military images. We nevertheless point out the following expressions, since they are rarer in the literature: "legiones dominicae" (*Mart. Saturn., Dativi,* and so forth) and "exercitus Christianus," "exercitus domini" (loc. cit. and *Mart. Quirini*).

.70. The destruction of idols by Christians also took place here and there before the time of Constantine. See Canon 60 of Elvira (ca. 300). The church disapproved of this behavior.

71. It appears that Christians took part in the uprisings in Melitene and Syria at the time of Diocletian (Euseb., *History* VIII, 6, 8). But this is not certain.

must keep his sword in its sheath, that he ought to die but may not kill.

In the fourth century it became otherwise. The heathen masses who poured into the church allowed themselves quickly to become fanatical for the new faith, and soon the holy war was proclaimed—not always with even the appearance of legal forms. One cannot deny that the *militia Christi,* as this concept had been cultivated in sermons and devotional literature, was a preparation for this turn of events. But to pursue and develop this theme lies outside of our task.

Yet it must be pointed out in this regard that even the war of Constantine against Maxentius, as well as the wars of Licinius against Maximinus Daza and Constantine against Licinius, was carried out unmistakably as a religious war. It was to be proved in battle who was stronger, the god of the Christians or the old gods. A few decades later, the Christian Firmicus Maternus in his book about the error of profane religions calls for fire and sword and demands of the emperors Constantius and Constans that they exterminate the heathen (chap. 20):

> Only a little more action and the devil will lie prostrate under the blows of your laws. . . . Raise up the standard of the faith; God has reserved this honor for you . . . raise up the banner of the law for men to revere; decree it, promulgate what is salutary! . . . Blessed are you also, for God has made you participants in his glory and will, and out of concern for his people Christ has reserved for your hands the rooting out of idolatry and the ruin of the temples of the profane. He has conquered evil spirits with spiritual arms, while you have conquered earthly evils. Raise up the trophies of victory and let the immense glory of the triumphs be displayed; rejoice in the downfall of profane things, rejoice with even greater faith. Your blessedness is joined with the power of God, for you have conquered for the salvation of man, Christ himself fighting with you.[72]

---

72. [*De errore profanorum religionum,* translated from the Latin.]

The *milites Christi* placed themselves at the emperor's disposal. The church, which had long since become a state within the state as a powerful episcopal confederation, inserted itself in the military and official order, all according to the design and will of the Christian emperors. It contributed in a major way to bringing under central control again the militarism which had threatened to destroy the empire in the third century. There were still uprisings by imperial pretenders in the fourth century, but if these were not as chronic and destructive as before, one needed to thank the "soldiers of Christ," that is, the church, which stood up for the unity of the empire.

2

The Christian Religion and the Military Profession

In the introduction to the previous chapter we briefly sketched the principles behind the relationship of the gospel as a message of peace to conflict and war. In what follows we shall concern ourselves with the concrete relationship to the military profession and the judgments made about it. What was offensive to the early Christians about this profession can be briefly summarized: (1) it was a warrior's profession, and Christianity on principle rejected war and the shedding of blood; (2) the officers, under given circumstances, had to pass the sentence of death, and the soldiers in the ranks had to carry out everything they were ordered to do; (3) the unconditional oath required of the soldier was in conflict with the unconditional obligation to God; (4) the cult of the emperor was at its strongest in the army and was hardly avoidable for each individual soldier; (5) the officers had to offer sacrifices, and the regular soldiers had to take part; (6) the military standards appeared to be heathen *sacra*; to reverence them was hence idolatry (in the same way, military decorations—wreaths and so forth—seemed idolatrous); (7) the conduct of soldiers in peacetime (their extortions, loose morals, and so forth) conflicted with the Christian ethic; (8) the traditional rough games and jokes in the army, for example, the *mimus,* were offensive in themselves and were connected in part with the service of idols and the festivals of the gods.

What position Christianity took with regard to the military

profession before the year 170 must be determined exclusively by conjecture based on later information. It is only from the time of Marcus Aurelius on that we possess direct sources which enlighten us about the actual relationships and how they were judged. The Christian documents of the earlier time are almost entirely silent.

This silence, however, is meaningful and instructive. In those documents we find discussion about the relationship to authorities and to the state, marriage and family questions of all sorts, the question of slavery, and a host of problems with regard to one's conduct in eating and drinking, socializing, dealings with the heathen. If a "military question" is completely lacking, there arises the well-grounded supposition that there was no such question at all in the Christian congregations at that time. The absence of the question, however, can have diametrically opposed grounds. It was either because Christians on occasion served as soldiers without blame, or because military service was self-evidently forbidden for Christians. Which is correct?

One would assume, a priori, that the first solution is most likely. No matter how self-evident the prohibition might be, there would have to be some defense against its violation in everyday life, and some traces of this struggle would be found in the earliest literature. But how could that be? Had Jesus not forbidden all revenge and retaliation for evil? Did he not teach complete gentleness and patience? And was not the military profession contemptible because of its extortions, brutalities, and its execution of tyrants' commands? Certainly; and because of this it follows without doubt that a Christian was not permitted to become a soldier voluntarily. The earliest Christians surely observed this rule, and it was not difficult for them to keep. There was no universal military obligation in the empire, and the number of troops was not large in comparison with the total population. The legions were recruited from volunteers. Only in very special cases of need were individuals forced into military service.[1] If the gaps in the ranks became too great, then by way of exception gladiators, slaves, barbarians, robbers, and riffraff were installed.[2] As a rule, the little people were able to avoid military service without any trouble. Consequently, there

---

1. Cf. Theodor Mommsen, *Römisches Staatsrecht* II, 2³ [1871–78], pp. 849–50; idem, "Die Konskriptionsordnung der römischen Kaiserzeit," *Hermes* 19:1ff.; Neumann, *Der römische Staat und die allgemeine Kirche* I (1890), pp. 127–28. Neumann writes, following Mommsen: "The legal military obligation of a Christian was naturally not given frequent attention in a time when the need for soldiers was met for the most part by volunteers. (Arrius Menander at the time of Septimius: 'For the most part the numbers were filled by soldiers who volunteered,' *Digest.* 49, 16, 4, 10.) There was only a relatively limited use of compulsory conscription under the Principate, although legally there was universal military obligation. We may note the wide expansion through voluntary enlistment in the formation of the army of Marius, also the very small numerical strength of the army in relationship to the extent of the empire, and the average fixed term of enlistment of twenty years, all of which made this possible. The Roman citizen with legal residence in Italy was excluded from military service from the time of Septimius Severus. One could become a soldier by voluntarily reporting for duty or by being conscripted or, finally, as a substitute for someone who was conscripted. Who was there to require the Christian who did not wish to serve to volunteer or to enter service as a substitute for someone else? Certainly a Christian might be conscripted, but then there would at least be the possibility of avoiding the onerous duty of personal service by finding a substitute." Concerning the relationship of the Jews to the Roman military, see Emil Schürer, *Geschichte des jüdischen Volkes im Zeitalter Jesu Christi,* I³, pp. 458–66. [4th ed., 3 vols. with index (Leipzig: Hinrichs, 1901–11); Eng. trans. *A History of the Jewish People in the Time of Jesus Christ,* 5 vols., trans. John Macpherson et al. (Edinburgh: T. & T. Clark, 1897–98); vol. 1 (newly translated) rev. and ed. Geza Vermes and Fergus Millar (Edinburgh: T. & T. Clark, 1973).] The Jews were free from Roman military service. That is certain for the time of Caesar (Josephus, *Antiq.* XIV, 10, 6); we may reasonably assume it for the time after that. The auxiliary troops conscripted in Judea came from the non-Jewish population.

2. This was already temporarily the case under Marcus Aurelius; but the rule still stood for a while that slaves were not allowed to be inducted into the army. (*Digest.* 49, 16, 11: "Slaves are prohibited from all forms of military service; they are punished rather through captivity.") This rule had something to do with the relatively late appearance of the "military question" in the church because the church probably originally included a large percentage of slaves.

was no conflict and no crisis threatening Christianity in this regard. No "military question" arose; the baptized Christian simply did not become a soldier!

It was different when the Christian religion penetrated the camp and soldiers were won to the faith. But even under these circumstances a military question need not immediately arise. The maxim of the Apostle Paul, "Everyone should remain in the state in which he was called" (that is, with his heathen marriage partner, in slavery, and so forth), could also be applied to the soldier. His profession might be relatively more offensive and dangerous than other worldly callings, but in principle there was no difference. Consider the dangers to the Christian way of life of a believer who was at the side of a heathen spouse day after day. For example, think of the difficulties facing a Christian wife of a pagan officeholder and judge! How terrifying were the dangers to which a Christian man who was a slave would always find himself exposed (to say nothing of a slave woman). Nevertheless, the wisdom of the great Apostle and of other missionaries had decided without hesitation that Christians should not dissolve these relationships. They were to remain within them, and one may assume, in the most extreme case, they would accept the consequences of their Christian profession by offering up their lives. As paradoxical as it may seem, one of the factors which enabled the missionaries to make this judgment was their certain expectation that the end of the world was near. Fanatics drew one conclusion from that expectation: "We will cast everything away and turn our backs on all worldly relationships." Thoughtful Christians, however, drew the opposite conclusion: "We will carry the burden which has been laid upon us, as heavy and difficult as it may be, for the short time which still remains." In this way, eschatology became a quietistic and conserving principle. It caused Christianity not to insist upon the carrying out of its principles in the state and in society, which would have led immediately to bloodshed or failure. It made possible a mission which could quietly lay its foundations. If one had told the first missionaries that the world would remain for a long, long time and Christ would not return for centuries, they would have lost that good conscience with which they now "in this last troubled time" let public matters simply go their way and within which they ordered their life in the smallest of circles. Opposition to the state, the ordering of society, public life, and so forth only became a matter of Christian conscience when Christians began to understand that they would have to deal with these conditions for a long time to come and would be responsible for them themselves. In the earlier time the contradiction between the ideal and present society was greater; it was so great that all comparison ceased, but the burden of practical tasks was experienced much less. Now, in the time of the Antonines, that contradiction lessened by several degrees, but the feeling of responsibility broke in with full force. How shall we relate ourselves as Christians to the world around us, with which we have become increasingly involved against our own will, since we, counting on its speedy demise, have done nothing to change it?

It is thus not surprising that there was no military question in the congregations until roughly the time of Marcus Aurelius. The baptized Christian did not become a soldier, and those who were converted to the Christian faith in the camp had to determine how they might come to terms with their soldier's life. We cannot forget that the control over these soldiers by the congregations could only be limited. Since the soldier was separated from civilian life much more than he is today, it was not easy for the congregations and their leaders to oversee him. But there was certainly great joy among the brethren when it was learned that even in the raw and brutal warrior's profession men had been awakened to faith. One would be more indulgent toward them than toward others; it was enough that the flag of Christ had been raised in the camp of the devil!

These considerations explain why there is hardly any early source material with regard to Christian soldiers and the church's judgment of them. The stories in the New Testament about the centurion at Capernaum, the centurion beneath the cross, and the centurion at Caesarea are not told in order to praise the military profession or even to suggest toleration. That they were soldiers in all these cases was of minor importance for the teller of the story. (Afterward, of course, these stories were exploited by some to the advantage of the military profession.) Similarly, we may conclude nothing about the recognition of the military profession from the comparison of the Christian missionary with the soldier who does not involve himself in civilian affairs (2 Timothy 2; see pp. 38–39 above). On the other hand, the glowing allusion to the discipline of "our" soldiers in the First Letter of Clement (see p. 40 above) seems to signify something more. The spokesman of the Roman congregation looks upon the Roman army with satisfaction and pride. Can he regard an army whose discipline and obedience he praises as in every respect the camp of the devil? I think not. The military profession was looked upon from two different perspectives, just as the emperor was. On the one hand Christians regarded the emperor as the accountable leader of the last world monarchy and therefore belonging to the devil's realm. On the other hand he was regarded as one who received the sword from God, who punished evil, and who delayed the final catastrophe. The soldier, then, insofar as he upheld order in the name of the emperor, was necessary and to be tolerated. But insofar as he served the devil's realm and spilled innocent blood, he was of the devil. Certainly no Christian could commend him, but just as the emperor here and there received a friendly word, so Clement here had one to spare for the soldiers.

More than this may be concluded from Luke 3:14. The

passage relates that soldiers came to hear the preaching of repentance by John the Baptist. "Soldiers also asked him, 'And we, what shall we do?' And he said to them, 'Rob no one by violence or by false accusation'"(RSV). What is informative is in the answer which John gives here, quite in conformity with what he says to the others—in particular, to the tax collectors. No flight from the world is demanded, nor from one's calling. What is required is simple morality. The special mention of the soldiers is striking, however, even if we think about Jewish soldiers in the army of Herod Antipas. But Luke did not write for Jews, hence not for Jewish soldiers. This may suggest that he wanted to say to his gentile Christian readers that a Christian soldier demonstrates his Christian calling by not engaging in robbery and extortion. If so, this is an expression of acceptance of the military profession under this condition. One may surmise that Luke is to be understood in this way. However, it is hard to remove the objection that it is not Jesus himself who says this, but his forerunner.[3]

That is all that we know about Christian soldiers until the time of Marcus Aurelius. Then the veil is rent, and for the period from 170 to 315 we possess considerable material. We begin our review with two apparently contradictory pieces of evidence. Celsus, the earliest literary opponent of the Christians, complains about them that just as they are generally un-Roman and unpatriotic so also they refuse to serve as soldiers of the emperor. At the same time, however, several writers testify that a number of Christians were to be found in the army of Marcus Aurelius, particularly in the Twelfth Legion.

Before we examine these and the other witnesses which follow, a question suggests itself. Did Christianity, conceived in its essentials, possess any kind of attraction, perhaps even

---

3. Clement of Alexandria comments on this passage that the Lord preaches through the mouth of John (*The Instructor* III, 12, 91).

a special attraction, for soldiers? At first glance it would appear that we must answer no to this question, and the first glance will, in this case, prove to be correct. It is quite clear that the Christian religion, whether we conceive it according to the sayings of Jesus, the teaching of Paul or James, the apologists or the Gnostics, would not possess any special magnetism for the average soldier. It was quite opposed to his métier. Yet not every soldier was an average soldier, and the Christian religion worked not only through its central powers of attraction but also through peripheral ones. Its freedom from every ethnic barrier, its universalism, its absolutism, the fact that it was not bound to any specific region, which enabled it to advance everywhere—all of this must be considered here. Above all, however, the strict monotheism, the teaching about one Lord of heaven and earth, must have commended itself to the soldier's spirit. This religion, which appears to be extremely complex to the thinker, was nevertheless capable of finding very simple expression. For its military followers, as they marched from place to place,[4] it was as omnipresent as the God they served. So the repelling and attracting powers might balance out, and in such cases, some of those who heard would follow the powers of attraction.[5] Christianity could not become a camp religion like the cult of Mithras and others. It set its ethical requirements too high for that and was too closely bound to its urban-episcopal organization. It remains to be seen whether in some provinces Christianity penetrated the army more deeply, contributing to the spread of the faith itself, and whether the Christian part of the army at the beginning of the fourth century did not become a still weightier factor in the relationship of state and church.

Let us return to the writers in Marcus Aurelius' day. Celsus

---

4. We have only to remember here the shifts in location of the legions.
5. We can also think of the attraction which the Christian religion must have had for soldiers because of the military speech and forms which it employed. (See the first chapter of this work.)

writes that if everyone did as the Christians, the emperor would be practically isolated and the realm would shortly be delivered into the hands of the wildest and most abominable barbarians.[6] Therefore, Christians should lend the emperor all possible aid, supporting him in fulfilling the obligations of his office, bearing arms for him, and when necessary, going into the field for him and leading his troops. He is assuming that Christians do not do this, and he undoubtedly has support for this assumption in the behavior of Christians known to him. Celsus was an admirable patriot and an excellent representative of old Roman officialdom, which, unfortunately, was more and more dying out at that time. He was deeply troubled by the condition of the empire, the attack of the barbarians, and the increasing difficulty in raising the necessary number of trained and equipped legions with which to oppose them. The proud words which Valerius Maximus had spoken about the army at the time of Tiberius were no longer valid: "I come now to the special glory and to the stability of the Roman Empire, which through a salutary perseverance has been preserved to this day safe and sound by the most tenacious bond of military discipline, in whose care and custody the serene and tranquil state of blessed peace rests" (*Factorum ac dictorum Memorabilium Libri IX,* II, 7, 1). Celsus wanted to see that state of affairs return and thought that Christians should help to achieve it. Instead of that, they were drawing back from the civil service and also from the army. He confirms what we have assumed, that the church did not allow its faithful to serve in the military.

At the same time, however, we learn that even then Christians were serving in the Twelfth Legion (*fulminata Melitensis*). It is credited to their prayers during a battle against the Quadi that a storm arose whose rainfall revived the parched Roman warriors. Even the emperor took notice of these

---

6. In Origen, *Celsus* VIII, 68, 73.

Christians' prayers.[7] It follows from this that the number of Christians in the legion was not inconsiderable. It would be surprising to find this in any other legion in the East at that time, with the exception perhaps of the *legio X Fretensis,* which was located in Syria. But the Twelfth had its quarters in Melitene and hence did its recruiting mainly from the regions on the upper run of the Euphrates. Edessa was there, and these regions constituted a center of Christianity at the end of the second century.[8] Those Christian soldiers came from these districts. They apparently regarded their God no differently from the way their comrades regarded theirs, namely as the great Ally, who must rush to their help in the extremities of war. The principled renunciation of military service on the part of the church cannot lead us to the false conclusion that there were no Christians in the army, as these facts indicate. The banner of Christ had been planted in the camp too, and the church must come to terms with this reality, which of course had its joyful side for Christians as well. The Christian writers not only did not condemn the soldiers who had called upon God in the midst of the dangers of war, but they rejoiced over it. They believed that God had hastened to help them and the Roman army and they gloried in this. That is quite significant. Christian rigorists would have had to wish rather that God had destroyed the whole army, thereby showing that he did not tolerate war.

---

7. For more particulars, see my treatment of this incident in the *Sitzungsberichte der königlichen Preussischen Akademie der Wissenschaften,* 19 July 1894. In spite of the writings to the contrary which my exposition has called forth, I consider it probable that Marcus Aurelius mentioned the prayer of the Christian soldiers in a communication to the senate. I am also convinced that soldiers from the Twelfth Legion were involved.

8. See my *Mission und Ausbreitung des Christentums in den ersten drei Jahrhunderten,* 1902, pp. 440ff., 468ff. [*The Mission and Expansion of Christianity in the First Three Centuries,* trans. James Moffatt (London: Williams & Norgate, 1908), 2:142ff., 192ff.] The royal house of Edessa became Christian around the year 200, and already in the course of the third century Christianity had penetrated Armenia. Also the neighboring Caesarea in Cappadocia was a main seat of the church. Concerning the point that the Melitene Legion still had Christians in its ranks later on, see below.

About two decades later Clement was writing in Alexandria and Tertullian in Carthage. They testify that Christianity had also made its way into the Egyptian and African legions. Clement does not express any disapproval of this. He treats the military profession like any other worldly profession in which a man is serving when he is apprehended by God's grace. (He follows St. Paul's way of thinking.) In *Exhortation to the Heathen* X, 100, he writes: "Practise husbandry, we say, if you are a husbandman, but while you till your fields, know God. Sail the sea, you who are devoted to navigation, yet call the while on the heavenly Pilot. Has (Christian— Harnack) knowledge taken hold of you while engaged in military service? Listen to the commander who orders what is right."[9] So one is to remain in his calling, including the soldier in the military, which is a profession like the others. Other passages in Clement (though not all) show that he regarded the military profession as impartially as he did any other.[10] He repeated the word of John the Baptist to the soldiers and gave to it the status of a dominical word. There may be Christian soldiers, then, if they keep themselves from robbery and extortion and listen to the voice of the heavenly commander.

Tertullian testifies plainly to the fact that Christians served in the army. He writes in the year 197 in his great *Apology* (chap. 37): "We have filled every place among you—cities, islands, fortresses, towns, marketplaces, the very camp . . ."[11] In response to the heathen reproach that Christians are enemies of the state, unfruitful dreamers, and comparable to Indian ascetics, he cries out, "We serve with you in the army!" (chap. 42).[12] Some years later, when he writes to the governor Scapula (chap. 4), he speaks about persecutions

---

9. [*ANF* 2:200.]
10. See *The Instructor* II, 11, 117; II, 12, 121; III, 12, 91.
11. [*ANF* 3:45.]
12. [So Harnack. *ANF* 3:49 has "fight with you." See Translator's Introduction, n. 13.]

which the *praeses legionis* has inflicted upon the Christians. This can only refer to the commander of the *legio III Augusta,* which was in Lambese; and since he only had jurisdiction over his soldiers, it follows that there were Christians in the Third Legion at that time.

But Tertullian is not candid with his heathen readers as he establishes the presence of Christians in the army. He writes as if he is quite in agreement with this state of affairs. In reality, however, he disapproves of it very strongly. With him we encounter for the first time the following line of argument: because a Christian may not enter the army, neither may he remain in it if he has received the gospel as a soldier—or if he remains, he must bear the consequences, rejecting everything that is contrary to his Christian profession, and so inviting certain death. Already in his treatise *On Idolatry* he states (chap. 19):

> But now inquiry is made about this point, whether a believer may turn himself unto military service and whether the military may be admitted unto the faith, even the rank and file, or each inferior grade, to whom there is no necessity for taking part in sacrifices or capital punishments.[13] There is no agreement between the divine and the human sacrament [Harnack translates "military oath"], the standard of Christ and the standard of the devil, the camp of light and the camp of darkness. One soul cannot be due to two masters—God and Caesar. And yet Moses carried a rod, and Aaron wore a buckle, and John (Baptist) is girt with leather, and Joshua the son of Nun leads a line of march; and the people warred: if it pleases you to sport with the subject. But how will a Christian man war, nay, how will he serve even in peace, without a sword, which the Lord has taken away? For albeit soldiers had come unto John and had received the formula of their rule; albeit, like-

---

13. In what precedes this quotation, Tertullian had shown that a Christian could not be a civil official because he may not judge in things which are a matter of life and death. That also decided the fact that he could not be an officer, since these judgments about capital crimes would arise.

wise, a centurion had believed; still the Lord afterward, in disarming Peter, unbelted every soldier. No dress is lawful among us, if assigned to any unlawful action.[14]

This speech leaves no room for doubt: one cannot serve God and the devil, one cannot serve God and the emperor! Therefore, no Christian is permitted to be a soldier, no soldier may become a Christian. And this applies not only during war, but also in peacetime. Tertullian had guarded against writing in this way in his communications intended for heathen readers. The treatise in which he says this was exclusively intended for Christians. We cannot exonerate this hot-blooded man from the charge of keeping two sets of books.

But there is something else noteworthy in this exposition. Obviously Tertullian does not represent here the general point of view of his Christian brothers. In a very clear way he even shows us the scriptural proofs which are used by the representatives of the opposing viewpoint. They appeal to Moses, Aaron, Joshua, and the wars of the people of God, also to the attitude of John the Baptist toward the soldiers, and to the centurion at Capernaum. Tertullian intends to get rid of the Old Testament instances easily with the remark that they are only presented by the opponents in jest. But why? Has not Tertullian himself in countless other cases simply appealed to the Old Testament? And if he knows of cases in which one is not permitted to do that, where is the boundary line to be drawn? He takes the New Testament witnesses more seriously. In fact, given the prevailing manner of using Scripture, they were very strong and really could not be refuted. But Tertullian opposes to these Scripture proofs another one: the Lord had disarmed Peter, had disarmed every soldier in Peter, and since this occurrence came later

---

14. [*ANF* 3:73.]

than the words of John to the soldiers and the conversion of the centurion, it is no longer permissible to appeal to those stories.

A rather artful proof. (The centurion from Caesarea is also forgotten, probably intentionally.) But the overpowering argument for Tertullian was not the setting of one scriptural proof against another. The overpowering argument was the objective fact that military service belongs in the realm of the devil and the emperor; hence no Christian can be a soldier.[15]

Some years later Tertullian addressed himself again and in a much fuller way to the theme of Christianity and the military. He dedicated one of his writings to it on the occasion of an event which was certainly not fictitious. Let us hear him speak (*De Corona* 1).

> Very lately it happened thus: while the bounty of our most excellent emperors was dispensed in the camp, the soldiers, laurel-crowned, were approaching. One of them, more a soldier of God, more stedfast than the rest of his brethren, who had imagined that they could serve two masters, his head alone uncovered, the useless crown in his hand—already even by that peculiarity known to everyone as a Christian—was nobly conspicuous. Accordingly, all began to mark him out, jeering him at a distance, gnashing on him near at hand. The murmur wafted to the tribune. . . . The tribune at once put the question to him, Why are you so different in your attire? He declared that he had no liberty to wear the crown with the rest. Being urgently asked for his reasons, he answered, I am a Christian. O soldier! boasting thyself in God. Then the case was considered and voted on; the matter was remitted to a higher tribunal; the offender was conducted to the prefects. At once he put away the heavy cloak, his disburdening commenced; he loosed from his foot the military shoe, beginning to stand upon holy ground; he gave up the sword, which was not nec-

---

15. Cf. also the "non milito" in *On the Pallium* 5.

essary either for the protection of our Lord; from his hand likewise dropped the laurel crown; and now, purple-clad with the hope of his own blood, shod with the preparation of the gospel, girt with the sharper word of God, completely equipped in the apostles' armor, and crowned more worthily with the white crown of martyrdom, he awaits in prison the largess of Christ. Thereafter adverse judgments began to be passed upon his conduct—whether on the part of Christians I do not know, for those of the heathen are not different—as if he were headstrong and rash, and too eager to die, because, in being taken to task about a mere matter of dress, he brought trouble on the bearers of the Name,—he, forsooth, alone brave among so many soldier-brethren, he alone a Christian. It is plain that as they have rejected the prophecies of the Holy Spirit, they are also purposing the refusal of martyrdom. So they murmur that a peace so good and long is endangered for them. . . . Now, as they put forth also the objection: But where (in Holy Scripture—Harnack) are we forbidden to be crowned? . . . as if it might be regarded as either no trespass at all, or at least a doubtful one, because it may be made the subject of investigation.[16]

In a very thorough presentation, Tertullian seeks next to show that wearing the wreath in any form and for any purpose is unlawful. When his opponents aver that he must make his case from scriptural proofs, he appeals to church tradition and to nature (wearing a wreath is contrary to nature). Still, he believes he can also discover negative witnesses in Holy Scripture with respect to wreaths. In the eleventh chapter he returns again to the special wreath, the soldier's laurel crown.

To begin with the real ground of the military crown, I think we must first inquire whether warfare is proper at all for Christians. What sense is there in discussing the merely accidental, when that on which it rests is to be condemned? Do we believe

---

16. [*ANF* 3:93.]

it lawful for a human oath to be super-added to one divine, for a man to come under promise to another master after Christ,[17] and to abjure father, mother, and all nearest kinsfolk, whom even the (Old Testament) law has commanded us to honor and love next to God Himself, to whom the Gospel, too, holding them only of less account than Christ, has in like manner rendered honor? Shall it be held lawful to make an occupation of the sword, when the Lord proclaims that he who uses the sword shall perish by the sword? And shall the son of peace (= the Christian) take part in the battle[18] when it does not become him even to sue at law? And shall he apply the chain, and the prison, and the torture, and the punishment, who is not the avenger even of his own wrongs? Shall he either keep watch-service ("stations") for others more than for Christ, or shall he do it on the Lord's day, when he does not even do it for Christ Himself? And shall he keep guard before the temples which he has renounced? And shall he take a meal where the Apostle has forbidden him (undoubtedly in or before the temples)? And shall he diligently protect by night those whom in the day-time he has put to flight by his exorcisms (namely the demons, which are identical with the idols in the temples), leaning and resting on the spear the while with which Christ's side was pierced? Shall he carry a flag, too, hostile to Christ? And shall *he* ask a watchword from the emperor who has already received one from God? Shall *he* be disturbed in death by the trumpet of the trumpeter, who expects to be aroused by the angel's trump? And shall the Christian be burned according to camp rule, when he was not permitted to burn incense to an idol, when to him Christ remitted the punishment of fire? Then how many other offenses there are involved in the performance of camp offices, which we must hold to involve a transgression of God's law, you may see by a slight survey. The very carrying of the name over from the camp of light to the camp of darkness is a violation of it.

---

17. "Respondere in alium dominum post Christum"; the expression is a military one. See Arrius Menander, *Digest.* 49, 16, 4, 10: "respondere ad dilectum" ("to answer to the summons of conscription").

18. Tertullian calls Christians "priests of peace" in *The Shows* 16.

Of course, if faith comes later, and finds any preoccupied with military service, their case is different, as in the instance of those whom John used to receive for baptism, and of those most faithful centurions, I mean the centurion whom Christ approves, and the centurion whom Peter instructs; yet, at the same time, when a man has become a believer, and faith has been sealed, there must be either an immediate abandonment of it, which has been the course with many; or all sorts of quibbling will have to be resorted to in order to avoid offending God, and that is not allowed even outside of military service; or, last of all, for God the fate must be endured which a citizen-faith has been no less ready to accept. Neither does military service hold out escape from punishment of sins, or exemption from martyrdom. Nowhere does the Christian change his character. There is one Gospel, and the same Jesus, who will one day deny everyone who denies, and acknowledge everyone who acknowledges God,—who will save, too, the life which has been lost for His sake; but, on the other hand, destroy that which for gain has been saved to His dishonor. With Him, the faithful citizen is a soldier, just as the faithful soldier is a citizen. . . . If one were to make an exception for the Christian as soldier, when for every Christian the command to openly confess the faith is binding even in the face of torture, one would overturn the essence of the sacrament of Baptism in a way that removed even the obstacle to voluntary sins. . . . Touching this primary aspect of the question, as to the unlawfulness even of a military life itself, I shall not add more, that the secondary question may be restored to its place. Indeed, if, putting my strength to the question, I banish from us the military life, I should now to no purpose issue a challenge on the matter of the military crown. Suppose, then, that the military service is lawful, as far as the plea for the crown is concerned.[19]

Tertullian now seeks to prove in particular how objectionable it is to receive and wear a military wreath. The wreath is always connected with one idol or another. "In these respects, the superstition of the military garland will be every-

---

19. [*ANF* 3:99–100. All words in parentheses here are from Harnack.]

where defiled and all-defiling."[20] The motives out of which the wreaths are distributed, the place, and the circumstances further demonstrate their heathen character. The Christian is not permitted to be a soldier, and if he were permitted, it would not be lawful to receive a laurel wreath. That is Tertullian's final word. By pointing to the behavior of the worshiper of Mithras (see p. 59 above), which should shame the Christian, he makes his point even more forcefully.

We can deduce much that is important from these passages: (1) Many Christians served in the African army.[21] (2) Some (perhaps many) left the military service after they became Christians. But that cannot have been the rule; most of them remained in the army. (3) Tacitly the congregations afforded them a certain kind of exceptional position with respect to Christian discipline. They were allowed to do what military discipline demanded, obeying the commands of their superiors and, especially in peacetime, carrying out the entire requirements of the service; these were regarded as something "external," as mere forms. (4) To support this kind of judgment, appeal was made to New Testament passages, for example, to the soldiers who came to John. (5) Christian soldiers had never before resisted military authority because of their profession of Christian faith.[22] (6) Tertullian's attack on Christians serving in the military was something new, unheard of before. As easy as it was for him to point out in principle the incompatibility of serving Christ with serving in the army (even in peacetime), he yet made no attempt to

---

20. [*ANF* 3:100.]

21. We are still unsure whether this fact can be used to explain the military coloration of several passages in the Old Latin (African) Bible translation. (See pp. 56–57 above.) We cannot clearly see the way in which that could have happened. But one may note that military expressions had worked their way into the African language itself (as they have in ours today). These would then appear in the Bible translation because the Latin Christians, as we have shown, regarded themselves as *milites Christi*.

22. Tertullian evidently knows of no precedent.

appeal to a prior, already established rigorist ethic and practice. His chief argument, that all Christians are already soldiers of Christ, was somewhat sophistical. (7) With regard to those who were soldiers already when they became Christians, he shows some uncertainty, which clearly proves that he had given up the game on this point in advance. He did not confront such Christian soldiers with the dilemma of leaving the military or dying as martyrs; rather he opened up for them a third possibility: to avoid contamination with heathen things to the best of their ability. (8) The special case which provided the occasion for Tertullian's writing is most remarkable. Why had the soldier only refused the garland and not resisted military authority before on any of a hundred other occasions? Perhaps he was a new convert or perhaps his conscience was suddenly stricken, but a different conclusion is more likely, particularly when we reexamine the last section of *De Corona*. Here is a Christian soldier claiming for his faith the same rights which his commanding officers would grant to him if he were a worshiper of Mithras. We must simply believe Tertullian that special consideration was given to the Mithras followers with regard to the military wreath. The Christians in the army, in particular this Christian, wanted a similar allowance to be made for them. This · soldier felt wronged in his religious practice because he was not permitted to do what the believer in Mithras could do with impunity. Regarded in this way, the little affair is not without significance. It is a symptom of the increased self-consciousness of the Christians (especially those in the army) as a religious group distinct from others. Apparently this Christian soldier did not at all want to demonstrate that Christian service and military service were irreconcilable. What he wanted to do was force the granting of the same privileges for Christians in the army which the followers of Mithras already enjoyed. In making the attempt he was destroyed.

There is something else of importance in Tertullian's words. He says that every Christian, even the civilian *(paganus)*, is a soldier of Christ, and every soldier of the emperor is in God's eyes a civilian.[23] Thus he lays the groundwork for the usage which distinguishes all Christians as *milites* from all other people as *pagani,* that is, civilians in the sight of God. This usage became widespread in the fourth century. (So *pagani* in Christian usage had nothing to do originally with people who lived in the countryside.) It is an especially clear proof of how dominant was the consciousness in the West that one became a soldier of Christ through Holy Baptism (the *sacramentum*). In the East that was not universally understood, which accounts for the mistaken meaning of *paganus* as having to do with the villages, a meaning which arose in the second half of the fourth century under the impression that the countryside remained heathen longer than the cities.

Tertullian's writing hardly changed any of the facts of the matter. Christians found themselves in the army after he wrote as they had before. Their numbers must naturally have increased with the growing number of Christians in the third century. But one thing is very clear: the feeling for the incompatibility of Christianity with the military profession was now coming forth more strongly in the declarations of some individuals. We already know the reason for this. Now for the first time Christians were really adjusting themselves to the world, and the question arose whether one could, so to speak, formally recognize the military profession and give it Christian accreditation. That had not happened earlier because Christians stood much too high above this question. But still another point needs to be considered. The esteem and credit of the military in the third century was diminish-

---

23. The expression *paganus* = "civilian" as opposed to *miles* is technical. See, for example, *Digest.* 49, 19, 14.

ing, to put it mildly. It was not high to begin with, and certainly the philosopher, with whom every Christian possessed a certain affinity, despised the military vocation. But now the army was becoming more and more a band of men about which no patriot could feel any joy. The shamelessness, the brutality, and the extortions of the soldiers knew no bounds.[24] Small wonder that the aversion was expressed more clearly in Christian circles too.

Although Origen once made a start at distinguishing necessary and just wars from frivolous and bad ones (*Against Celsus* IV, 82), he forbade Christian participation in the military entirely, as Tertullian did.[25] "We are come," he wrote (*Celsus* V, 33), "agreeably to the counsels of Jesus, to 'cut down our hostile and insolent "wordy" swords into ploughshares and to convert into pruning-hooks the spears formerly employed in war.' For we no longer take up 'sword against nation,' nor do we 'learn war anymore,' having become children of peace, for the sake of Jesus, who is our leader, instead of those whom our fathers followed."[26] Also very instructive in this regard is the argument presented in VII, 26. Origen pursues the thought here that the constitution and laws of the people of Israel could not have remained unchanged had they received the gospel. "For Christians could not slay their enemies, or condemn to be burned and stoned, as Moses commands, those who had broken the law."[27] He then proceeds in a remarkable way, saying that in olden times it was necessary to give the Jews the right to this kind of behavior, for if they had not been permitted to defend them-

---

24. Christians had, moreover, complained about denunciations by soldiers. See Tertullian, *To Scapula* 5.

25. It is noteworthy that Origen delivered theological lectures, by request, to the commander of the *Legio III Cyren.* in Bostra (Euseb. *History* VI, 19).

26. [*ANF* 4:558.]

27. [*ANF* 4:621.] Later, however, the church did so!

selves, they would quickly have been vanquished by their foes. But just because of this, the same Providence which at that time gave permission to wage war had to decide to let the Jewish state perish and give to the divine on earth a new form. Now the church is here, which does not carry the sword but becomes stronger the more it is persecuted. The deciding argument, however, is found in VIII, 70, 73. Celsus (see p. 73 above) had invited Christians to follow the Roman state and also to serve in time of war. Origen answered that the reverse should obtain. "But if all the Romans, according to the supposition of Celsus, embrace the Christian faith, they will, when they pray, overcome their enemies, or rather, they will not war at all, being guarded by that divine power."[28] We render aid to the emperor by means of our spiritual armament through our prayers. But we remind those who would compel us, for the common good, to proceed into battle and to kill, that even their own priests are not placed among the soldiers, because God must be worshiped with pure hands. If that is reasonable, how much more reasonable is it that we, while others go to war, take part as priests and servants of God in the campaign, by keeping our hands pure and by praying for the legitimate king and his victory. We render an even greater service to the kings than the warriors in the field insofar as we overcome by our prayers the demons, who provoke the war and destroy the peace. "And none fight better for the king than we do. We do not indeed fight under him, although he require it; but we fight on his behalf, forming a special army—an army of piety—by offering our prayers to God."[29]

Origen uses many words, and for him they are not merely words; but what stands out clearly is the revolutionary refusal, "We do not fight even though the emperor requires

28. [ANF 4:666.]
29. [Against Celsus VIII, 73; ANF 4:668.]

it." Thus one could speak under Philip the Arabian; even a Tertullian had not dared to say as much. Some decades later Lactantius said the same (*Institutes* VI, 20, 16), extending it to every "just man." "Thus it will be neither lawful for a just man to engage in warfare, since his warfare is justice itself, nor to accuse anyone of a capital charge, because it makes no difference whether you put a man to death by word, or rather by the sword, since it is the act of putting to death itself which is prohibited."[30] We find the same principle enunciated in the old church canons, which we possess today only in reworked form.

> Persons who have the authority to take life or soldiers shall not kill anyone, even if they are commanded to do so. . . . They shall not wear any crown on their heads which they receive as a decoration. Anyone in an outstanding position of leadership or who possesses a ruler's authority and does not keep himself disarmed, as is fitting for the gospel, shall be separated from the flock. . . . Let no Christian become a soldier (when it is not necessary for him to do so).[31] A superior who has a sword shall not bring bloodguilt upon himself. If he has shed blood he shall not participate in the mysteries until he is purified through correction and tears and groans.[32]

But these instructions of the moralists were in no way followed in the third century. Not only do many particular facts speak against it, but there are also voices like that of Eusebius, who in his *History of the Church* (VIII, 14, 11) rebuked Maximinus Daza not only for leading his officers on to theft and avarice but also for weakening the army through revelry. That presupposes a certain appreciation of the army on the part of Eusebius. This attitude in Christian circles from Clement of Rome (see p. 40 above) to Eusebius is also

---

30. [*ANF* 7:187.]

31. The phrase in parentheses is most probably a later addition.

32. *Canons of Hippolytus* 13, 14. Early and late material is interlaced here. [Translated from Harnack's German.]

evident when we consider that the distinguished Christian teacher Julius Africanus treats tactics in an unembarrassed way in one of his works. So Christianity already possessed a military writer at the beginning of the third century.[33] We will assemble the historical facts next. They cast a bright light on the relation of Christianity to the military profession and teach us much that does not come to the fore in the discussion of this question as a matter of principle.

The martyrdom of a maiden named Potamiaena created quite a sensation in the year 202/3 in Alexandria. Eusebius relates the story in detail from a rather good source in his *History* (VI, 5). Here we learn that the soldier Basilides, who led her to her death, protected her from the insults of the mob and showed his sympathy for her in a spirited way. Potamiaena thereupon promised him that she would pray to the Lord for him and that he would soon be rewarded for what he had done for her. Her words and her steadfast endurance of martyrdom made such an impression on the soldier that when, soon thereafter, he was required to swear an oath in a lawsuit, he explained to his fellow soldiers that he could not, because he was a Christian and a Christian may on no account swear. At first they took it for a joke, but as he remained firm, they led him to the judge. Here he made his steadfast confession and was put in prison. He told the Christians who visited him there that Potamiaena had appeared to him three days after her martyrdom. She had placed a crown upon his head and said that her prayer to God on his behalf had been heard; the Lord would soon take

---

33. The voluminous work to which we refer here was called "Κεστοί"; a large part of it was devoted to tactics. This encyclopedic work covering all kinds of knowledge was certainly not characteristic for Christian writing. In fact, we are astonished when reading some of the fragments in our possession that an important Christian teacher could write as he did. I would have printed the parts concerning military science in the appendix if they were available in a good edition, but they still await the publisher. [Harnack's appendix of texts is in any case deleted here.]

him to himself. He was baptized in the prison and beheaded the next day.

The story is like a little novel. It is instructive that the soldier, after he had decided to become a Christian, immediately renounced any oath taking, but in so doing faced certain death. Where Christians were numerous in a regiment, as soldiers or (later) as officers, consideration was often given to their religious faith, but not even an officer could free someone from taking an oath in a civil suit. Earnest-minded Christians were in any case more endangered in the army than in any other profession, as the relatively great number of attested martyrs proves. They fought and fell as *milites Christi.* The soldier who led a Christian to execution (or was the informer) and then became a Christian himself gradually became a stereotype in the Acts of the Martyrs.[34] This was not always legendary; such cases must have recurred. (Cf. the noncommissioned officer Pudens in the *Acts of Perpetua,* chap. 9.) It is also attested, for example, that in the Alexandrian persecution under Decius, a soldier named Besas protected the accused Christians from the insults of the mob as Basilides had done; he also was beheaded. (See Dionysius Alexander in Eusebius, *History* VI, 41, 16.)

The following passage from the thirty-ninth letter of the great Bishop Cyprian sheds light on the spread of Christianity in the military in Africa before Cyprian's time. In order to recommend a certain Celerinus, a confessor of the Carthaginian congregation, for acceptance into the clergy, he writes:

His grandmother, Celerina, was some time since crowned with martyrdom. Moreover, his paternal and maternal uncles, Lau-

---

34. From an earlier time, see the legend about the death of James the son of Zebedee in Clement of Alexandria (retold by Eusebius, *History* II, 9). Clement claimed to know from a "tradition" that the man who delivered up James was beheaded with him, after he had been moved by the steadfastness of the apostle and was converted.

rentius and Egnatius, who themselves also were once warring in the camps of the world (*castra saecularia*), but were true and spiritual soldiers of God, casting down the devil by the confession of Christ, merited palms and crowns from the Lord by their illustrious passion. We always offer sacrifices for them, as you remember, as often as we celebrate the passions and days of the martyrs in the annual commemoration.[35]

We have here a formal dynasty of martyrs: grandmother, uncles, and nephew. Both uncles served in the army and suffered death for Christ as soldiers; the "once" is not to be interpreted that they were soldiers at some earlier time. Cyprian wants to say that it was through their courageous Christian confession that they left the secular military service. Celerinus evidently had his origins in the military camp on his father's and his mother's side. Tertullian was the son of a subaltern officer. One sees that Christianity had penetrated the African army and that the military provided the church with excellent warriors.[36]

A still greater spread of Christianity[37] is shown by an episode from the persecution under Decius in Alexandria, which is reported to us by the contemporary Dionysius of Alexandria (Eusebius VI, 41, 22–23). As the Christians stood before the judge and were accused, a little squad of soldiers stood nearby.[38]

And as a certain person who was being tried as a Christian seemed inclined to deny, they standing by gnashed their teeth, and made signs with their faces and stretched out their hands, and gestured with their bodies. And when the attention of all

---

35. [This letter is number 33 in *ANF* 5:313.]

36. As a Christian rhetor, Cyprian naturally rejects war totally; see the biting word in *Ad Donat.* 6. Lactantius does the same; see *Inst.* I, 18, 8; V, 17; VI, 20.

37. One must guard against generalizations, however.

38. Σύνταγμα στρατιωτικόν from the *Legio II. Traian. fortis.*

was turned to them, they rushed up to the tribunal saying that they were Christians, so that the governor and his council were affrighted. And those who were on trial appeared most courageous in prospect of their sufferings, while their judges trembled. And they went exultingly from the tribunal rejoicing in their testimony (μαρτυρία—their impending martyrdom?—Harnack); God himself having caused them to triumph gloriously.[39]

The conclusion is not quite clear. I suspect that their martyrdom is meant, because it is hardly conceivable that the judges, even though momentarily frightened and intimidated, would let the rebellious soldiers get away. Be that as it may, it is certain that the whole little band of soldiers were Christians, or sympathizers, who in the critical moment came forth on the side of the Christians. Since it appears from this account that one was not able to intentionally exclude Christian soldiers in order to protect a judicial proceeding directed against other Christians, we have a measure of how widespread the Christian religion was in this Alexandrian unit and how determined these Christian soldiers were to place their religion above military discipline. The little episode bespeaks volumes. If it looked like that in Egyptian regiments as early as the year 250, we cannot be amazed at what Constantine did sixty years later when he ordered the cross attached to the Roman standards before the battle at the Milvian Bridge.

The same Dionysius relates (in Eusebius VII, 11, 20) that the persecution was directed against men and women, young and old, maidens and aged wives, soldiers and civilians. Thus he particularly emphasizes the persecution of soldiers. That also occurs elsewhere, apparently because legal proceedings

---

39. [*A Select Library of Nicene and Post-Nicene Fathers,* second series, ed. Schaff and Wace (New York, 1890; reprint ed., Grand Rapids: William B. Eerdmans Publishing Co., 1953) (hereafter, *NPNF*), 1:285.]

against soldiers as Christians were especially numerous, as numerous as those against the clergy. Epiphanius says as much in relation to the persecution under Diocletian (*Panarion* 68, 2): "Among the fallen one was a soldier, the other a cleric, namely priests, deacons, etc."

Eusebius tells a story which is worthy of attention from the time of peace after the Valerian persecution (hence around 260) (VII, 15). In Caesarea, a respected officer named Marinus received a higher rank because of his seniority. The officer next in line came forward and complained that according to the old laws[40] Marinus could not be given rank in the Roman army because he was a Christian and did not offer sacrifice to the emperor; the position belonged instead to him. The judge asked Marinus what his convictions were. He firmly confessed himself a Christian and was thereupon given three hours to think it over. As he left the judgment hall, Bishop Theoteknus came up to him, began a conversation, took him by the hand, and led him into the church. There at the altar he drew back Marinus' cloak, and, pointing on the one hand to the sword which he wore and on the other to the Gospel book, he bade him choose. Without hesitating, Marinus reached out his hand toward the Holy Scripture. The bishop said to him, "Hold fast to God, and strengthened by him mayest thou obtain what thou hast chosen, and go in peace."[41] Just then the time of grace elapsed. Marinus repeated his confession before the judge and was executed. The account is interesting because it shows that even a Christian officer, and certainly a common soldier, could remain in the army unopposed at first. Without doubt, his superiors knew Marinus was a Christian as well as his

---

40. We do not know what special laws are meant here; probably special imperial orders that no Christian officers were to be tolerated in the army.
41. [*NPNF* 1:303.]

accuser did. They would also have known that he did not offer sacrifice.[42] Not only did they wink at this, they even wanted to promote the officer. But when a formal charge was made (and how simple that was if the rival could disregard the odium of being an informer), it was all over for him. No one could protect him anymore because the law spoke against him. That is how things went even in a time of peace;[43] how much worse it must have been in a period of formal persecution of the Christians!

That was revealed most clearly in the last great persecution under Diocletian and his co-emperors. The persecution began in the military; the ranks of the soldiers, and especially the officers, had to be purged of Christians. Eusebius puts it matter-of-factly (VIII, 1, 7): "This persecution began with the brethren in the army."[44] A few chapters later he provides more precise information (VIII, 4): "He (the devil—Harnack) did not wage war against all of us at once, but made trial at first only of those in the army. For he supposed that others could be taken easily if he should first attack and subdue these." That is a beautiful testimony to the strength of commitment of Christians in the army and shows at the same time that they were not in fact blamed by the church for their occupation as soldiers. He continues, "Thereupon

---

42. With some justification we may conclude from this that consideration was sometimes shown to Christians in the army and they were not expected to do that which was offensive to them. The matter in question is sacrifice to the emperors. Marinus said that he was a Christian and did not offer sacrifice to the emperors. These words did not contain the basis for two accusations but only one.

43. In spite of this, the church never produced general or specific instructions for the behavior of the Christian soldiers; the matter was impossible to regulate. Very characteristic in this respect were the canons of the Synod of Elvira in Spain (ca. 300). They were concerned mainly with the regulation of the Christian life in the heathen environment, but with regard to the soldier's occupation they kept a studied silence.

44. [*NPNF* 1:323.]

many of the soldiers were seen most cheerfully embracing private life, so that they might not deny their piety toward the Creator of the universe." The commander-in-chief[45] allowed them to choose between offering sacrifice and quitting the military.[46] Most chose the latter. "And one or another of them occasionally received in exchange for their pious constancy, not only the loss of position, but death[47] . . . (yet) the multitude of believers, as it is likely, made him afraid, and deterred him from waging war at once against all."[48] Lactantius gives us further information (*Of the Manner in which the Persecutors Died* 10). We learn that it was the powerful but superstitious Emperor Galerius who instituted the measures. He feared that he would suffer the wrath of the gods and military defeats if he tolerated Christian soldiers in the army any longer. In addition there was a specific cause: the diviners in the army—the emperor frequently consulted the gods—blamed the presence of Christians at the sacrificial rites for their unpropitious findings when they examined the animal sacrifices. Lactantius does not deny the presence of Christians, and, he adds triumphantly, they had indeed disturbed the rites, that is, they had made the sign of the cross, thereby driving away the demons and bringing about the unhappy results of the divination. That is instructive! The Christian officers naturally made the sign of the cross in order to protect themselves from the demons and still be able to take part in the ceremony as Christians. Evidently they had done so for a long time. We see here under what con-

---

45. In his *History,* Eusebius does not give the name, but in his *Chronicle* (for the year 2317) he names Veturius. "Commander of the army Veturius persecuted the Christian soldiers, the persecution against us having begun gradually from that time to the present."

46. So much consideration is being shown. It concerned officers, after all, not common soldiers.

47. That is not so remarkable; the simple dismissal is much more remarkable.

48. [*NPNF* 1:326.]

venient conditions a Christian soldier could participate in a sacrificial rite at that time! There must have been a quiet arrangement, so to speak, between the church and the military administration. The Christian officer was present at the sacrifice but made his sign of the cross; with that, both sides were content. Galerius, who took his religion seriously, destroyed this arrangement. He directed that all officers and even the common soldiers should sacrifice, and if they refused, they would be dismissed from the military. He sent this order in writing to all the commanding officers. "With this measure he contented himself at first."[49] But as things were, such a mild measure would no longer be tolerated; the Christians were already too numerous. One must either withdraw the command or go farther, carrying out the battle across the whole line. Galerius soon decided on the latter course and attempted to win over the aging Diocletian to this fateful plan. A battle was waged against the whole church and all the Christians in the following decade in the East. (It was much weaker in the West.) But within that battle the struggle concerning the army was always clearly prominent. The last great battle, which ushered in the new historical epoch, came to a head in the question whether the army should remain true to its religious traditions or, by tolerating Christianity, renounce them. This question stood along with the other about church and state. Should one attempt to demolish the powerful organization of the church in the last hour, so to speak, or should one quietly watch as this organization by its sure advances rendered ineffective the laws and administration of the state? Diocletian's persecution was the ill-fated answer to these questions.

We lack statistical evidence concerning the numbers of

---

49. [*ANF* 7:305. Harnack footnotes this sentence in Latin:] "Thus far his rage and wrath proceeded, and no one did anything more against the law and religion of God."

Christians in the army. Eusebius appears to regard the Twelfth Melitene Legion as almost entirely Christian (V, 5, 1). But one can understand him in a different way, and what obtained in this legion is not to be seen as standard for the others (see p. 74 above) since its recruitment territory was in great part Christian by the year 300. Legends like those about the Thebaic Legion belong entirely in the realm of fable and are to be disregarded.[50] But the politics of Galerius and, as we shall see, Constantine and Licinius make it quite probable that the number of Christians in some legions, including officers, was quite considerable.

There are a good number of Acts concerning soldier martyrs which come from the last persecution, but few of them are reliable. The *Acts of Nereus and Achilleus,*[51] *Polyeuktes,*[52] *Typasius,*[53] and so forth are to be laid aside.[54] The following Acts are instructive: Julius Veteranus at Durostorum in Moe-

---

50. See Albert Hauck, *Kirchengeschichte Deutschlands* I[2], p. 9, n. 1; p. 25, n. 1 [5 vols., 1887–1920]. I agree with the writer concerning the spread of Christianity through the army in Gaul, Germany, and elsewhere. (Even among the Goths it will not have been captive Christian soldiers, but rather captive citizens and farmers, in particular, Cappadocians, who planted Christianity.) One needs to be cautious, however, with what Hauck says about the incompatibility of the Christian confession and military service.

51. Achelis, *Texte und Untersuchungen zur Geschichte der altchristlichen Literatur* [Leipzig, 1893] XI, 2.

52. He belonged to the Melitene Legion. See Conybeare, *The Apology and Acts of Apollonius* (1894), pp. 123ff.

53. *Analecta Bollandiana* 9 (1890): 116ff. My judgment about this piece of writing was entirely too favorable in *Chronologie* II, pp. 481–82. [Harnack, *Geschichte der Altchristlichen Literatur bis Eusebius,* Teil II: *Die Chronologie,* Band 2: *Die Chronologie der Literatur von Irenäus bis Eusebius,* 1st ed. (Leipzig: J. C. Hinrichs Verlag, 1897); expanded ed., introduced by Kurt Aland (Leipzig: J. C. Hinrichs Verlag, 1958).]

54. From the "Acts of Dasius," which are not completely reliable (*Analecta Bollandiana* 16 (1897): 5ff.), one learns about the celebration of the Saturnalian feast in the army. See Parmentier in the *Rev. de philol.* 21 (1897): 143ff. and Wendland in *Hermes* 33 (1898): 175ff. Wendland and, most recently in a somewhat different way, Reich (*Der König mit der Dornenkrone,* 1904) have brought in the mocking of Christ by the soldiers here. —The *Acta Archelai* begin with a military legend in praise of Marcellus in Carchar. This rich Christian once purchased 7700 *(sic)* prisoners

sia (at the time of the Great Persecution),[55] Maximilian at Tebessa in Numidia (12 March 295),[56] and Marcellus at Tingis in Mauretania (on 30 October after the beginning of the reign of Herculius Maximian and before the Great Persecution).[57]

The *Acts of Maximilian* appear at first glance to be a striking witness that Christians at that time regarded their Christian profession and military service as irreconcilable. Maximilian, who is the son of a veteran and as such is obliged to serve, declares repeatedly that he cannot become a soldier because he is a Christian. But on closer inspection we discover the following: (1) The father of Maximilian is himself a Christian; still, he expected that his son would not resist entry into the military; he had already purchased a uniform (a new garment) for him. (2) The judge remonstrates with the young man, telling him that Christians serve as soldiers *in sacro comitatu* (in the sacred bodyguard) of Diocletian and his co-emperor. Maximilian does not contradict this; rather he remarks, "They must know what is best for them; I am a Christian and I will not serve." Undoubtedly he disapproves of those Christians who serve in the army, but the fact remains. The Christian father rejoices in his steadfast son, but he himself remains in the army.

---

of war from the soldiers. That made a deep impression on them. "Astounded with admiration for the man's extraordinary piety and generosity which they enjoyed, and overcome by his example of humane kindness, most of them were led to join the faith of our Lord Jesus Christ by casting away the military belt; others made off to their own camp after little more than a fourth part of the money had been paid, while almost all the rest took as much as they needed for their journey and departed." The story is in all probability an invention, but still not without worth.

55. *Analecta Bollandiana* 10 (1891): 50ff. Perhaps prepared according to the protocol.

56. The Acts rest on the court protocol; printed in Ruinart, *Acta Mart.* (Regensburg, 1859), pp. 340–41.

57. Ibid., pp. 343–44. See the appendix for these three martyrs. Still to be mentioned are the Acts of Sebastian, Sergius and Bacchus, and Apadius.

From the *Acts of Marcellus* we learn that the heathen rev-
elries carried on at the birthday of the emperor led to a
Christian officer taking off the uniform which had become
burdensome to him and bearing the consequences of this
act. Marcellus is described as a centurion in the *Legio
Traiana*. It must be identical with the *Legio II Traiana,* which
was usually quartered in Alexandria. There was no legion
stationed in Mauretania Tingitana.

We also learn from the *Acts of Julius the Veteran* that there
were exceptional cases, when Christian soldiers so perceived
their Christian calling that military service became unendur-
able for them. (Julius had served twenty-seven years in the
army and participated in seven campaigns.)

A certain Pachomius served in the army of Constantine
against Maxentius. The love that was evidenced by Christian
soldiers was said to have led him to Christianity. He then
became a monk and was the founder of the famous colony
of monks in Tabennisi.[58]

We have finally to consider Seleukus, about whom Eusebius writes in his work on the Palestinian martyrs. He suffered the death of a confessor along with Pamphilus.

> He was from Cappadocia by birth, had distinguished himself
> in the military service, and had reached an important rank.
> Then, long before the martyrdom, he acquired fame by his
> frank confession and his endurance of hard blows. Happily,
> he managed to be released from his military position. As a
> true soldier of Christ he then dedicated himself to the care of
> orphaned children, lonely widows, and those afflicted by pov-
> erty and sickness. He ruled over them like a bishop. He was
> a father and a helper who alleviated the sorrows and griefs of
> the outcasts. Finally, he was permitted to suffer the death of
> a martyr.[59]

---

58. *Vita Pachomii.*
59. *Texte und Untersuchungen* XIV, 4 [Leipzig, 1896], pp. 77ff., 96ff.
[The translation is from Harnack's German. Cf. *NPNF* 1:353.]

This picture which Eusebius presents of the former officer is an attractive one. What is important to note is that Seleukus received his separation from the military because of his Christian faith. Hence the break with the army was not always violent (see p. 94 above); Christian officers also left military service by simple dismissal.

In the campaign against Maxentius, Constantine decided to lift up the cross with the initials of Christ as a military standard. In this way the Christian religion would not only be tolerated but raised above all religions.[60] The epoch-making shift from paganism to Christianity first occurred in the army. It was from here that public recognition of the Christian religion took its start. Constantine could hardly have taken the step if there had not been a considerable number of Christians in his army and if the army had not already grown accustomed to the fact of Christianity in its midst. (That there were even priests in the camp cannot be concluded with certainty from *Life of Constantine* I, 32.) The victory of the emperor over Maxentius set the seal on his deed. "By virtue of this salutary sign, which is the true test of valor, I have preserved and liberated your city from the yoke of tyranny. I have also set at liberty the Roman senate and people, and restored them to their ancient distinction and splendor" (Eusebius, *Life of Constantine* I, 40).[61] *Christus victor!* The Christian God had revealed himself as a God of war and victory!

It is not within the limits of our present task to tell how the church judged this deed, what the emperor did further for its benefit, and in what manner the church obliged him. But what happened now with respect to the military profession is of the highest importance. The church passed the following decree at the great Council of Arles in 314 (Canon

---

60. Eusebius, *Life of Constantine* I, 26ff.
61. [*NPNF* 1:493.]

III): "Those who throw down their weapons in peace shall be excluded from communion" ("De his qui arma proiciunt in pace placuit abstineri eos a communione"). This decree appears so surprising and offensive to some historians that they have attempted to give a meaning to the phrase "throw down their weapons" which it cannot have. They argue that *arma proicere* must equal *arma in alium conicere*, so the canon says no Christian may carry weapons of war in peacetime! But this interpretation is quite impossible. Others quite arbitrarily replace the words *in pace* with *in bello*. Still others assume that war is not being talked about here at all, but rather gladiatorial games. But the words and their most obvious interpretation in my opinion remain unshaken: the church at Arles not only disapproved of the hitherto occasional (*öfters*) practice of desertion by Christian soldiers on account of their faith, but went so far as to place it under the fearful punishment of excommunication. By doing this the church achieved and proclaimed the full union of state and emperor with Christianity and church in the military sphere. To be sure, the words *in pace* create difficulties. One can understand them to mean "in times of peace," but one can also think of the peace which now prevailed between the empire and the church. It can be argued against the second meaning that this sense does not arise immediately from the words. Nevertheless, I prefer it (with Aubespine, Hefele and others), because in the first case *in pace* appears almost superfluous. I do not think we can be certain about this.

At any rate, the church by this decree fundamentally revised its previous theoretical position concerning the army and war. It was able to do so because Christian practice had for a long time led the way and because the *arma proicere* of Christian soldiers had not been the rule before, rather the exception. Now it was forbidden under heavy penalty. The Christian soldier would not be excluded from the church if he remained in the army; such exclusion had never been the case even before this time. He faced excommunication if he left the army, for whatever reason. The union of church and state on this ground could not be more intimate. The church made common cause with the emperor to keep the soldiers with the flag.

But the emperor was also obliging to the church. In a decree he commanded as follows:[62]

> Once more, with respect to those who had previously been preferred to any military distinction, of which they were afterwards deprived, for the cruel and unjust reason that they chose rather to acknowledge their allegiance to God than to retain the rank they held [see p. 94 above]; we leave them perfect liberty of choice, either to occupy their former stations, should they be content again to engage in military service, or after an honorable discharge, to live in undisturbed tranquillity. For it is fair and reasonable that men who have displayed such magnanimity and fortitude in meeting the perils to which they have been exposed, should be allowed the choice either of enjoying peaceful leisure, or resuming their former rank.

This matter could not have been arranged in a more honorable way for those concerned.

Licinius had made common cause with Constantine on the Christian question in the beginning. According to the account of Lactantius,[63] he conducted the war against Maximinus Daza as a war to decide between Christianity and paganism. Maximinus' great animosity to the church forced him to this. Before the battle he had copies of a prayer distributed to the soldiers. It was allegedly given to him at night by an angel. We do not know who the clergyman was who was hiding behind the angel, but he was undoubtedly the earliest

---

62. The form of this decree is known to us from *Life of Constantine* II, 33. The emperor published it after the conquest of the East as far as Palestine. [*NPNF* 1:508.]

63. *On the Manner in Which the Persecutors Died* 46.

military chaplain. The prayer is Christian if not outspokenly so. It is the first Christian military composition which we possess, the root of all Christian army and battle songs. It reads:[64]

> Supreme God, we beseech thee;
> Holy God, we beseech thee;
> Unto thee we commend all right;
> Unto thee we commend our safety;
> Unto thee we commend our empire.
> By thee we live, by thee
> We are victorious and happy.
> Supreme, holy God, hear our prayers;
> To thee we stretch forth our arms.
> Hear, holy supreme God.

The army was transformed into a Christian army by this battle song. It took the place of heathen invocations and sacrifice, and it must be compared with them if one would properly evaluate its significance. How widespread must the Christian religion have been within the army, even if in a strangely diluted form, for Licinius to undertake this experiment! Victory came to him as it had to Constantine on the Milvian Bridge.

But now began the conflicts between the previously friendly and victorious emperors. The West was too small and limited for Constantine. His reputation as the emperor first designated by the Christian God prevented Licinius from establishing himself in a similar way. So he saw himself thrown back on the side of paganism and took upon himself the role of opposing once again the old gods to the new religion with which Constantine stood in league. The first move was naturally to purge the court and the corps of of-

---

64. The Christian nature of the song could be doubted; but the invocation "Holy God" next to "Supreme God" at the beginning and the end appears to me certainly to indicate Christianity. [*ANF* 7:319.]

ficers of Christians once more. "At length he threw off the mask, and gave orders that those who held military commissions in the several cities of the empire (hence, the police and security officials first—Harnack) should be deprived of their respective commands, in case of their refusal to offer sacrifices to the demons."[65] The war which now broke out with Constantine became again a contest to decide who was stronger, Christ or the old gods. (See p. 99 above.) Constantine triumphed. After this victory, the complete harmony between the army and the Christian religion which already existed in the West was achieved in the East. Some have erroneously understood the Twelfth Canon of Nicaea as expressing the incompatibility of Christianity and the military profession.[66] Against this view it is sufficient to refer to Hefele (*Konzil-Geschichte* I[2], pp. 414ff.).[67] The canon does not concern the military profession in general and its relationship to the Christian religion; rather it concerns those Christian soldiers who at first lived up to their confession by leaving Licinius' army when he issued his commands against Christianity. Then, however, because of hunger or lust for spoils, they returned to his army. It is understandable that the church could not simply allow these men to continue as its members. They had been treacherous and had taken part in the anti-Christian measures of Licinius.

---

65. *Life of Constantine* I, 54 [*NPNF* 1:497]; *History* X, 8. In this time the attested martyrdom of forty soldiers from the Twelfth Melitene Legion took place. We still possess their remarkable *Testament*. See Bonwetsch, *Neue kirchliche Zeitschrift* III, 12, pp. 705ff. The testament itself does not indicate that it originated with soldiers. We see here again that it is the Melitene Legion which produced so many confessors.

66. [The canon reads, "Those who endured violence and were seen to have resisted, but who afterwards yielded to wickedness, and returned to the army, shall be excommunicated for ten years etc." (*NPNF* 14:28).]

67. Cf. also my *Mission und Ausbreitung*, p. 395 [*Mission and Expansion*, 2:63–64].

After the victories of Constantine there was no longer any barrier dividing the *milites Christi* from the army. On the contrary, the church itself required these "soldiers of Christ," if they served in the army, to remain in the army. The church even created warlike saints for them (alongside the warlike archangels), and henceforth turned over to the monks its earlier notions about war and military service. The church threw itself into the arms of the emperor. He exercised command over the Christian priests and the Christian soldiers. In fact, it was only the Christians who were now considered "soldiers" in the higher sense of the word. The rest were *pagani,* "civilians." But the unity for which Constantine strove, and which seemed for a moment to be realized, did not endure. Within the Christian state the church sought to win back its independence. New tensions developed and within them the old questions about the military reappeared in a new form.

Addenda

To pages 81, 84: In his lectures which have just appeared (*The Church's Task under the Roman Empire,* Oxford, 1905, p. 42) Bigg supports the meaning of the word *paganus* which we have given here. He writes: "'Paganus' means 'a civilian' as opposed to 'a soldier' (Pliny, *Epp.* X, 18: 'et milites et pagani' ['both soldiers and civilians'], cf. Juvenal. XVI, 33; Tacit., *Hist.* I, 53; III, 24, 43, 77; Tertull. *De Cor.* 11), and is used in a general sense like our 'layman' (Pliny, *Epp.* VII, 25: 'as in our camps, so also in our literature, there are more who are in civilian dress *(cultu pagano)'*). In this sense the word is found, perhaps for the first time, in Persius, *Prol.* 6: 'I myself, a semipagan, bear our song to the sacred festivities of the inspired prophets.' The first instance of the use of 'pagan,' as opposed to 'Christian,' is to be found possibly in an inscription of the second century given by Lanciani, *Pagan and Christian Rome,* p. 15: 'She was faithful *(fidelis)* among the faithful, among the aliens she was a pagan *(pagana)*,' which from the use of the word *fidelis* is most probably Christian, not Isiac or Mithraic." One may suppose that the followers of other religions in the Roman Empire (especially those which used military images, as did the religions of Mithras and Isis) called those who were not initiated *pagani.* This would have prepared the way for the later Christian usage. It would be groundless to suppose, however, that the Western Christian designation of Christians as *milites* is to be explained as due to the influence of other religions. Spontaneous parallel developments occur in the history of religion much more frequently than the researchers of today are accustomed to assume. Instead of explaining C from B, one ought to look first for an A (similar conditions) from which both B and C can be derived.

To chapter 2: We have seen that we may not determine the position of the church with regard to the military simply according to the judgments of the theologians, particularly the rigorists. Here should be added the witness of the ceremonial prayer of the church. In this prayer "brave armies" were requested for the emperors. Tertullian himself (*Apol.* 30) has to testify to that: "Without ceasing, for all our emperors we offer prayer. We pray for life prolonged; for security to the empire; protection to the imperial house; for brave armies, a faithful senate, a virtuous people, the world at rest" [*ANF* 3:42]. Cf. Cyprian, *Ad Demetr.* 20: "We always ask for the repulse of enemies and we pour forth our prayers constantly and urgently for your peace and safety." Arnobius, IV, 36: "For why indeed have our writings deserved to be given to the flames, our meetings cruelly broken up, in which prayer is made to the Supreme God, peace and pardon are asked for all in authority, for soldiers, kings, friends, enemies, etc." [*ANF* 6:488]. And *Acta Sebastiani:* "By the prayers of Christians the state itself is made better and prospers, for Christians do not cease praying for your empire and for the safety of the Roman army (*pro salute Romani exercitus*)." On the other hand, one should not overrate the significance of the prayer of the church for our question, because (1) Christians also prayed for enemies, (2) one could conceive of the *salus Romani exercitus* in different ways, (3) insofar as brave armies were requested for the emperors, the prayer was a part of the "rendering unto Caesar." The emperor had, however, even purely from an apocalyptic standpoint, a certain divine right to exist in opposition to the barbarian hordes and anarchy; for the *pax terrena* was also from the strictest Christian standpoint a relative good in connection with the wished-for *mora finis* (delay of the end). But in order to maintain the *pax terrena* the emperor needed soldiers. They belong to the "sword," which Paul (Rom. 13:4) had already recognized as a godly attribute of authority and which no father of the church had dared flatly to deny to the emperor.

[Note by Harnack following the appendix:] To my knowledge we do not possess any inscriptions from the pre-Constantinian period in which the deceased is identified as a Christian and as a soldier. But we may draw no conclusion from this about the sparse number of Christian soldiers, for they certainly never or only very rarely put their military rank on inscriptions.

Index of Passages

Revelation
33ff.
2:10—35

Apadius, Acts of—97

Archelaus, Acts of—96-97

Arles, Canon III—99-100

Arnobius
Against the Heathen
II, 5—60
IV, 36—106

Arrius Menander—67

Catech. Rom. II, 1, 2—30
II, 3, 2—30

1 Clement 21, 37—40-41, 70,
87

Clement of Alexandria

Exhortation to the Heathen
X, 100—75
XI, 116—45

The Instructor
I, 7, 54—45
I, 12, 98-99—46
II, 11, 117—75
II, 12, 121—75
III, 12, 91—71, 75

The Stromata VII, 16, 100—45

*Who Is The Rich Man That
Shall Be Saved?* 25, 34—46

Excerpta ex Theodoto 85—45

Commodian
Instructions II, 11, 12—60-61

Cyprian

Ad Demetr. 20—106

Ad Donat. 6—90

Epistles
3, 3—61
10, 1, 2—60-61
15, 1—60
28, 1-2—60-61
28, 2—60-61
30, 6—61
31, 4-6—60-61
39—89-90
43, 5—61
46, 2—60-61
54, 1—60-61
58, 4, 8, 10—60-61
59, 13—61
60, 2—60-61
61, 2-3—61
69, 8—61
76, 4—60
76, 6—60
77, 2—60

Damasus
Letters—60

Dasius, Acts of—96

Digest. 49, 16, 4, 10—67, 80
49, 16, 11—67
49, 19, 14—84

Date Due